THE MEDIEVAL WORLD

Mike Corbishley

Illustrated by James Field

PETER BEDRICK BOOKS
NEW YORK

TIMELINK: MEDIEVAL WORLD

Published in 1993 by

Peter Bedrick Books
2112 Broadway
New York, NY 10023

Designed and produced by Lionheart Books

Artwork by James Field.

Published by agreement with Reed Consumer Books, London, England.

Library of Congress Cataloging-in-Publication Data
Corbishley, Mike.
The medieval world / Mike Corbishley. -- 1st American ed.
(Timelink)
Includes index.
Summary: Surveys the known world between 450 and 1500. Discusses Buddhism, Islam, Vikings, the Crusades, plague, medieval towns, and more.
ISBN 0-87226-362-2
1. Middle Ages--History--Juvenile literature. I. title. II. Series.
D117.C66 1993
956--dc20 92-31445 CIP

Printed in Hong Kong

Acknowledgements
Designer: Ben White
Project Editor: Lionel Bender
Text Editor: Mike March
Picture Researcher: Jennie Karrach
Media Conversion and Typesetting:
Peter MacDonald and Una Macnamara
Managing Editor: David Riley
All maps by Hayward Art Group.

Picture credits
Page 3: Michael Holford. Page 11: Bodleian Library, Oxford (Ms Douce 217.Fol 12V.) Page 12: English Heritage. Page 15: Michael Holford. Page 21: Sonia Halliday and Laura Lushington. Page 23: e.t. archive. Page 25: Ancient Art and Architecture Collection. Page 26: e.t. archive. Pages 28, 33: Michael Holford. Page 34: Explorer, Paris/Hervé Negré. Page 37: Michael Holford. Page 39, left: English Heritage. Page 39, right: e.t. archive. Pages 41, 44: Michael Holford. Page 47: Bibliotheque Royale Albert 1er, Bruxelles, Ms 13076-77, fol. 24 verso. Page 51: Sonia Halliday Photographs.

Constructing a cathedral tower in a town in France in the 12th century – see pages 52 and 53.

CONTENTS

Left: A carved stone erected by Viking King Harald in about 980 – see pages 28 and 29.

INTRODUCTION

This book is an introduction to the greatest events in world history from the end of the Roman Empire in western Europe to the first voyages of Europeans to the New World of the Americas. It is divided into seven chapters arranged in time sequence from AD 450 to 1500. Each chapter includes an overview of world events, short features on, for instance, important civilizations and major battles, and extended features on a variety of subjects of special interest. These include, among others, the rise of the Islamic religion, the Vikings and the medieval town.

The Medieval World is the second title in the Timelink series, which is designed to give young readers an overall view of different peoples and their histories, and the links between civilizations across the globe. Obviously, the book cannot show the whole history of the medieval world, but it does show many of the significant turning points – the great events that changed the way people lived then and have influenced the way we all live today.

Throughout **Timelink: The Medieval World** there are maps, illustrations, diagrams, photographs and timecharts. The maps show the migrations, or movements, of people, the spread of civilization and empires, and the voyages of discovery. The

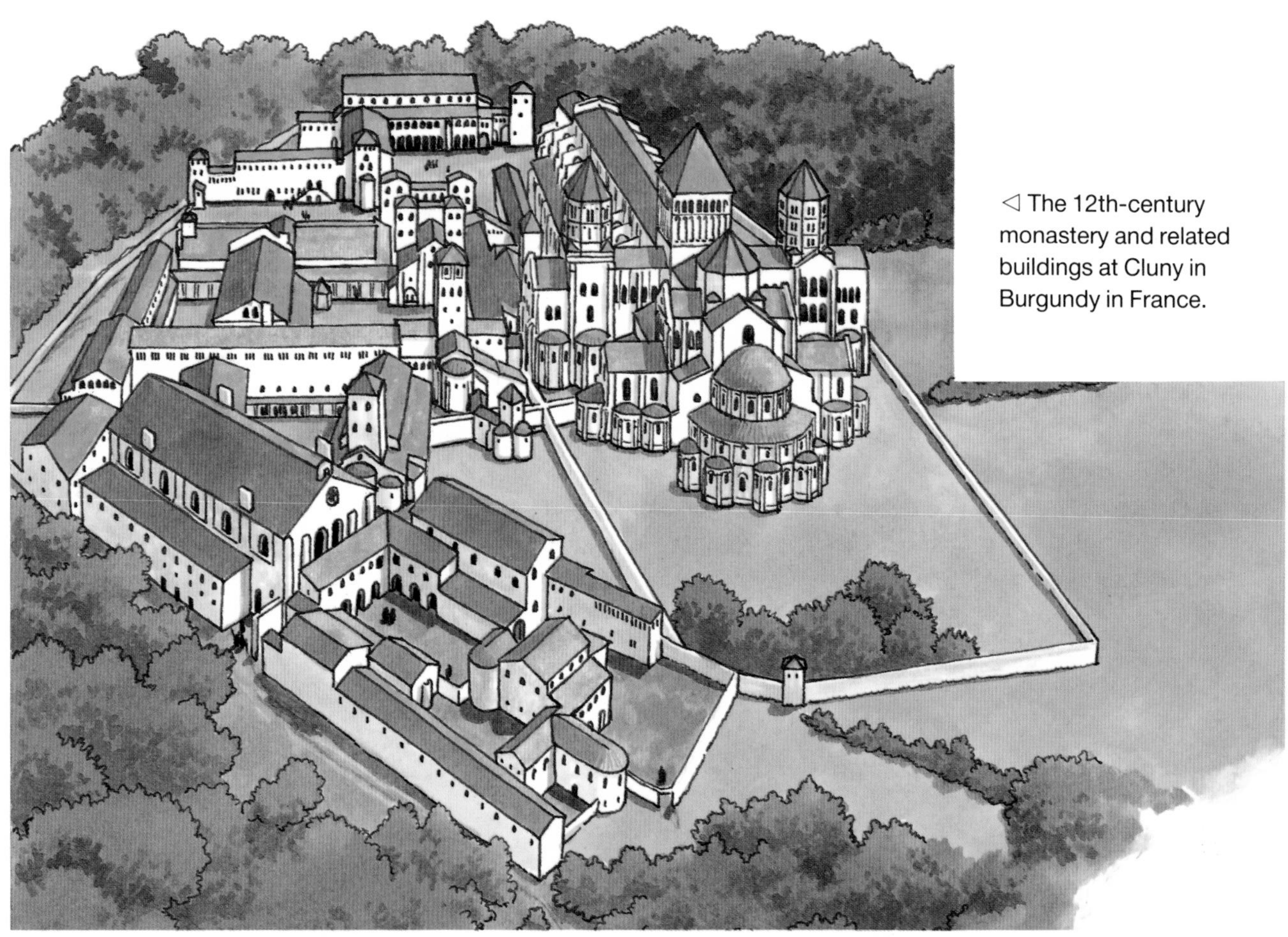

◁ The 12th-century monastery and related buildings at Cluny in Burgundy in France.

illustrations show how people lived – their clothes, their farms and their houses – and include reconstructions of the towns, temples or churches that formed part of their world. The timecharts list the dates of important events around the world. At the back of the book are two larger timecharts covering the whole of the medieval period, for quick, easy reference, and a Glossary of unusual words, which are also explained in the text.

Finding out about the medieval world

How do we know what happened hundreds of years ago? Usually we can build up a picture of everyday life in the past by collecting and piecing together all the evidence of the period, rather like a detective at the scene of a crime.

There are two sorts of evidence. First, there are all the objects actually left behind – clothes, weapons, tombs and other buildings. We call these objects archaeological evidence. Second, there are the written records. Historians, who study and write about the past, can also read and interpret these written records to try to work out what sort of lives people led. In this book, you can study that evidence, in words and pictures, and make up your own mind about the effect of the great events in medieval history.

A NOTE ABOUT DATES

All the dates in this book are based on a calendar which has the birth of Jesus Christ as its starting point. Events occurring before that date are counted backwards from it – Before Christ, or BC for short. Events happening after the birth of Christ are counted forwards from it. They are given the letters AD, from the Latin words *anno domini*, meaning 'in the year of the Lord'. In this book, all the dates are AD unless it says otherwise.

The Dark Ages

You will often come across the term 'Dark Ages' in history books, describing the early medieval period. The word 'dark' was chosen by historians because there are few written records surviving for those peoples who invaded and helped to destroy the Roman Empire in the west – peoples whom the Romans called 'barbarians'. This period, which is where this book begins, was also considered 'dark' because there was little archaeological evidence left to discover – or so it was thought. In fact, more is being discovered about these 'dark age' peoples and their civilizations, and you can read about it here. They were not all barbarians, and many, including the Vikings, produced beautiful works of art. For this reason, the term 'Dark Ages' is not used in this book.

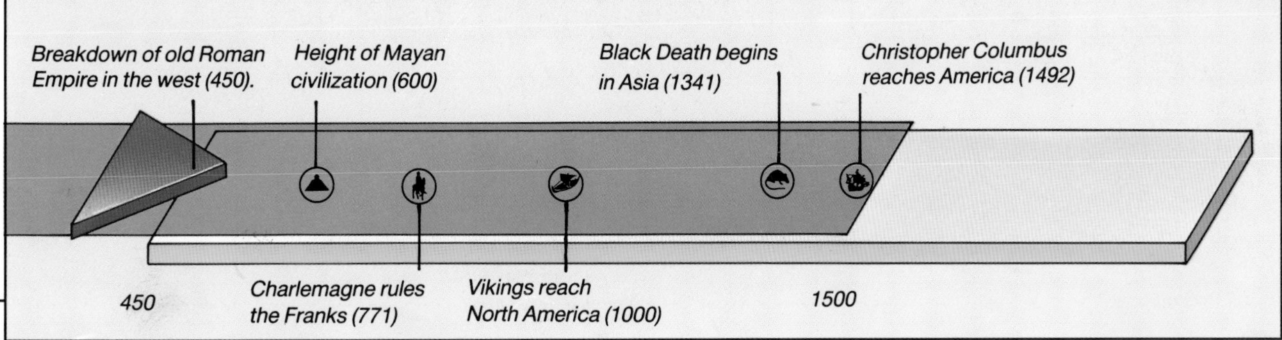

THE CHANGING WORLD

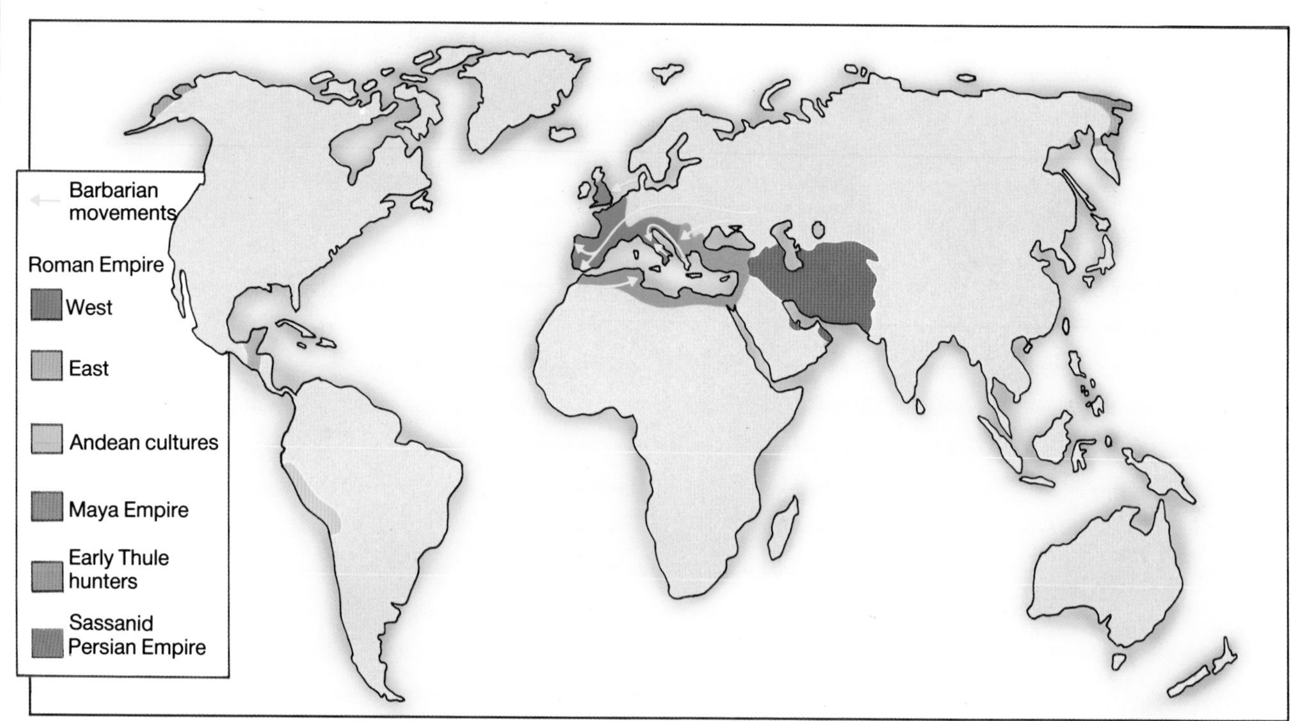

▲ WARRING KINGDOMS, NEW EMPIRES 450–600

Around the Mediterranean, new peoples were moving into the territory of old empires, such as the Roman Empire. On the other side of the world, hunters began to migrate into North America, while farther south new civilizations, such as the Mayan, were in control.

▼ THE SPREAD OF RELIGION 600–950

Two religions, Christianity and Islam, dominated the Mediterranean area and the Middle East. Conquering Muslim armies clashed with the Byzantine Christians. In the Far East, Buddhism became the most important religion. In northern Europe the Vikings set sail in search of new lands.

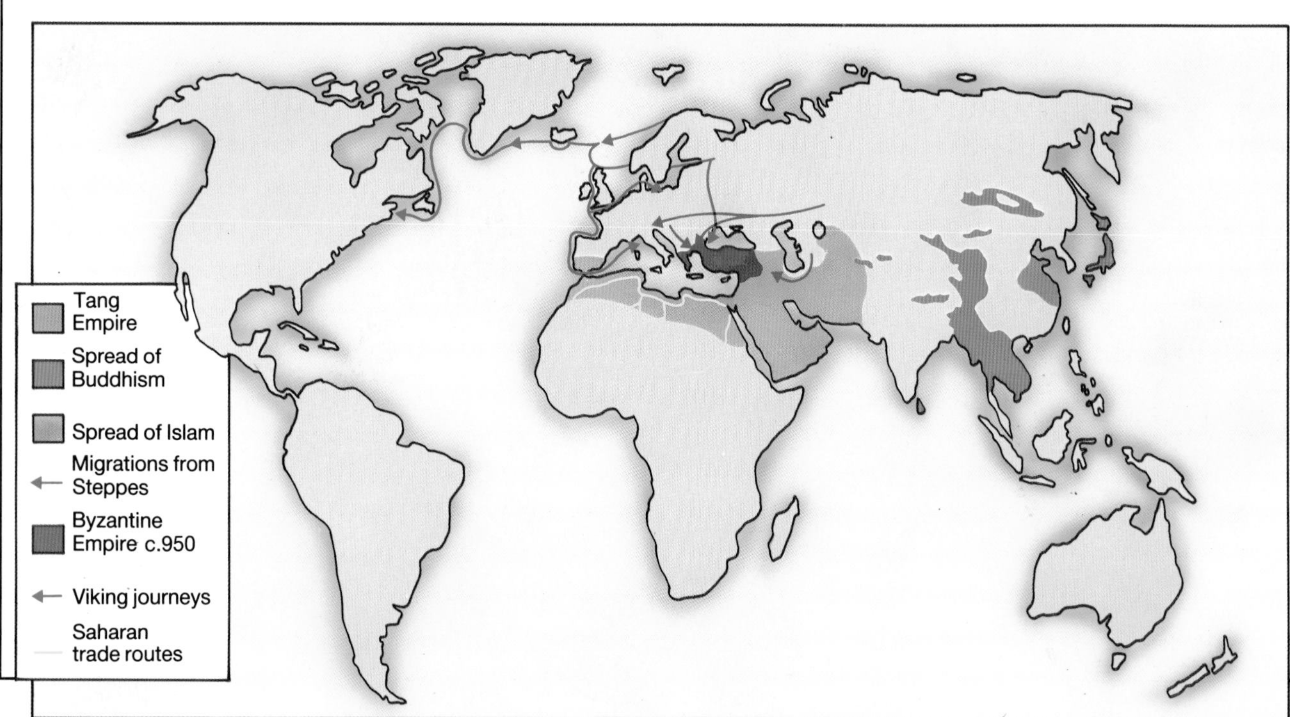

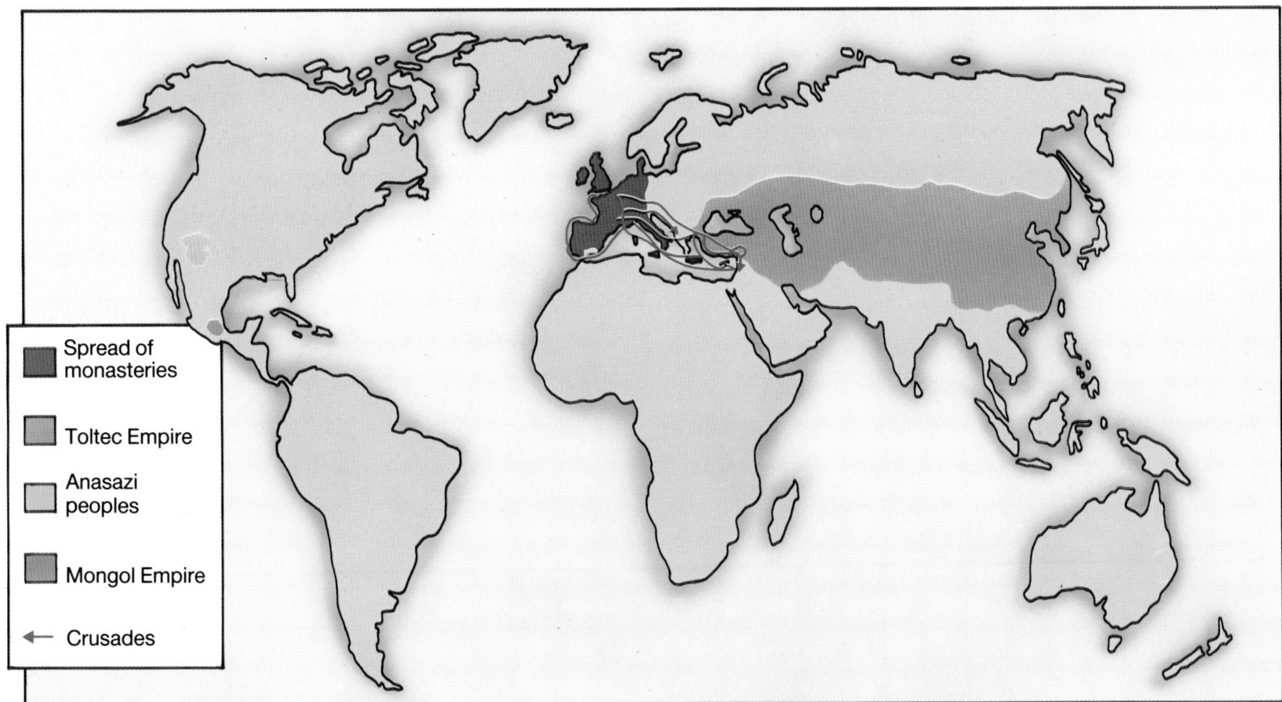

Ⓐ EMPIRE BUILDING 950–1250

The continuing conflict between Christianity and Islam led to the great Crusades to conquer the 'Holy Land'. Farther east, a new force – the Mongols – campaigned and conquered to build the world's largest empire. In the Americas, the Toltec civilization became a powerful force.

Ⓥ DISCOVERY, WAR AND PLAGUE 1250–1500

The terrible plague known as the Black Death ravaged both Europe and Asia. Rebellions sprang up in Europe, followed by major wars. At about the same time, Europeans also began to discover the rest of the world – Africa, the Far East and the Americas.

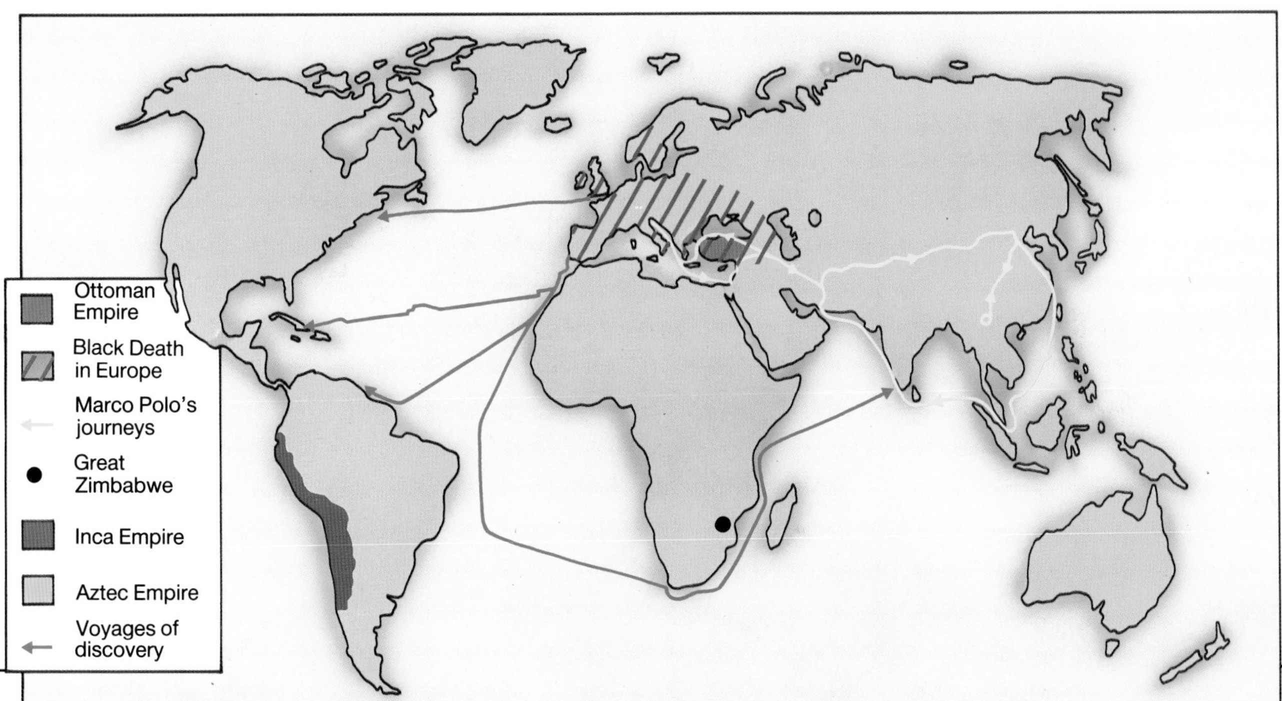

EMPIRES UNDER ATTACK

By the 5th century, throughout Europe and the Mediterranean, the world as people had known it was changing rapidly. Large numbers of people were restless and on the move, looking for new lands to settle or simply looking for booty. The civilizations that had been established for centuries were being threatened.

This was also true of India and the Far East. Like the Roman Empire, India was menaced by tribes beyond its borders, and as a result the Gupta civilization (see page 13) eventually broke down into a number of warring kingdoms. Farther east, in China the invading Toba Wei people reunified the north, while across the Pacific Ocean in Mesoamerica – the lands between North and South America – the city civilizations were expanding rapidly and building magnificent temples (see Teotihuacan, page 13).

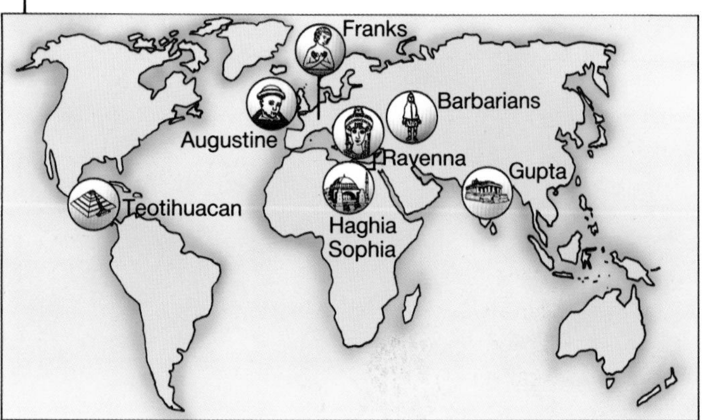

BARBARIAN MOVEMENTS

During the 4th and 5th centuries the lands around the Mediterranean Sea were disturbed by great movements of peoples – some seeking new lands to live in, others seeking war. The Roman Empire, which had originally been ruled by the Emperor in Rome, now had two capitals – Rome in the west and Constantinople in the east. The Eastern Roman Empire survived into the medieval period although the territory it controlled became smaller. Hordes of invading peoples swept across the Roman Empire. One Roman writer described the Gothic peoples as 'suddenly descending like a whirlwind...ravaging and destroying everything in its path'. These newly-arrived peoples soon built their own way of life and established their own kingdoms.

▷ Migrations of 'barbarian' peoples sometimes began with small groups settled outside Roman towns, or sometimes, like the Saxons, they were brought into the towns for military protection. 'Barbarians' from the east came in huge numbers and overwhelmed the established civilizations.

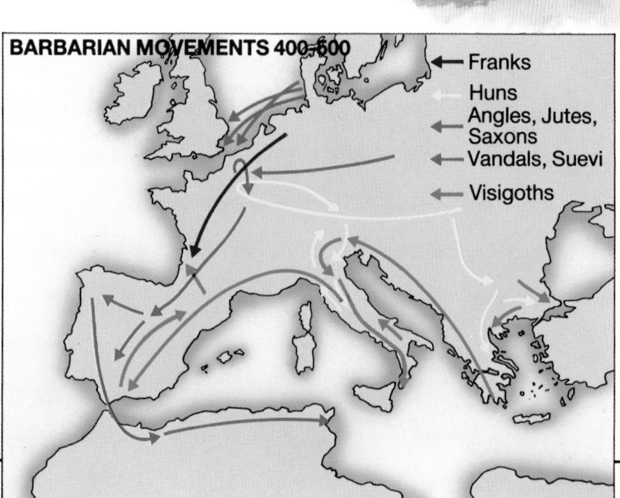

△ Not all migrating peoples could be justly called 'barbarian'. This illustration, taken from a late 5th-century Roman mosaic floor in the city of Carthage in North Africa, shows a man wearing the dress of a Vandal riding outside his country house – a typical Roman building.

450–500

c450 Saxons, Angles and Jutes begin to settle in Britain.
451 Attila the Hun's forces defeated.
455 Rome sacked by Vandals.
475–6 Romulus Augustulus last Roman Emperor in the west.
476 Odovacar the German becomes King of Italy.
480 Huns invade Gupta Empire in India.
484 Huns kill Persian Sassanian Emperor.
488 Ostrogoths under Theodoric invade Italy.
c500 Period of Six Dynasties begins in China.
c500 Thule hunters arrive in Alaska and spread across the northern Arctic to Greenland.

500–600

c500 Farming introduced into the forests of Brazil from the Amazon area.
520 Theodoric begins building Church of San Vitale in Ravenna.
533 Emperor Justinian's campaigns against the Vandals.
535–54 Ostrogoths conquered in Italy by Eastern Roman Empire.
537 Church of Haghia Sophia consecrated.
552 Southern Spain retaken by Justinian.
552 Buddhism introduced into Japan.
565 Justinian dies.
581 Sui Dynasty reunites China.
597 Augustine's mission to England.
c600 Invading Huns in the east are forced back by Persians and Turks.
c600 Mayan civilization at its height.

Decline of the Roman Empire

In the year 330 the Emperor Constantine moved the capital of the Roman Empire from Rome in the west to Constantinople (today Istanbul, Turkey) in the east. Sixty-five years later, the Empire was split into eastern and western halves. But by the 5th century the Empire – east and west – was being threatened by invading hordes of peoples whom the Romans called 'barbarians'. The outer provinces, such as Britain and Gaul, were attacked, as Angles and Saxons pushed west to seize new lands.

In 410 Rome itself was occupied by Alaric, the chief of the Visigoths. Originally, the Goths – Visigoths and Ostrogoths – had come from the steppes of Russia. Another group whose name struck fear into Roman hearts were the Huns, who settled just north of the River Danube on the Roman frontier.

THEODORIC AND RAVENNA

Ravenna, an important Roman port in north-east Italy, was captured in 493 by Theodoric, the king of the Ostrogoths. He was an educated Christian who had been brought up in Constantinople. During his reign he put up a number of very fine buildings in his capital, Ravenna, including the Church of San Vitale which was begun in 520. Later, Ravenna and the rest of Italy was recaptured by the Eastern Roman Empire and the Emperor Justinian completed the building of the church. The drawing below is from a mosaic showing Theodoric's wife, the Empress Theodora making a gift of a golden chalice to the church.

The Christian Empress Theodora

JUSTINIAN AND HAGHIA SOPHIA

There were many magnificent buildings in Constantinople, the capital of the Eastern Roman Empire. Among the most beautiful was the church of Haghia Sophia, meaning Holy Wisdom. Built by the Emperor Justinian and consecrated as a church in 537, it had a high dome in its center with two half domes on two sides. The huge building looks rather solid from outside, but the decoration inside, with light streaming in through the dome windows and with colored mosaic walls and ceilings, gave the appearance of something beyond this world. In 557 an earthquake damaged the dome but it was rebuilt even taller than the original.

Haghia Sophia, Constantinople

THE ROMAN INFLUENCE

By the middle of the 5th century the western provinces of the Roman Empire had many different peoples living in them who destroyed the Roman way of life. But here at the Roman city of Viroconium (now called Wroxeter), on the border between England and Wales, the ruined city was revived by the late 5th century and Roman ways continued even when Britain was no longer a Roman province. The city center was rebuilt in the Roman style, but in wood and plaster. The main building shown here could have been the mansion of the city's ruler, an Irish chieftain called Cunorix, whose tombstone was found just outside the city's defenses.

The town of Wroxeter in the late 5th century

W. ROMAN EMPIRE

c450 Saxons, Angles and Jutes settle in Britain.
451 Huns defeated in north-eastern France.
455 Rome sacked by the Vandal king, Geiseric.
475–6 Romulus Augustulus last Roman Emperor in the west.
476 Odovacar becomes king of Italy.
486 Clovis, King of the Salian Franks, defeats the Roman Synagrius.
488 Ostrogoths under Theodoric invade Italy.
493 Odovacar defeated and killed by Theodoric, who establishes his capital at Ravenna.
511 Clovis, recognized as King of the Franks, dies.
520 Theodoric begins building the Church of San Vitale in Ravenna.
526 Death of Theodoric.
560 Irish monk Columba founds a church on Iona, Scotland.
568 Lombards invade Italy.
597 Augustine sent by Pope Gregory to England.

E. ROMAN EMPIRE

468 Failure of Emperor Leo's expedition against the Vandals.
527 Justinian crowned emperor with his wife Theodora.
532 Riots against Justinian in Constantinople.
533 Campaigns against 'barbarians' in Africa and Italy.
534 Attacks by Slavs and Bulgars.
535–54 Ostrogoths conquered in Italy.
537 Church of Haghia Sophia consecrated.
538 The Byzantine Empire attacked by Bulgars.
539-40 Attacks by Huns. A second wave follows in 559.
549, 551 Attacks by Slavs.
552 Byzantines succeed in reoccupying southern Spain.
561 Peace treaty signed with Persian Emperor Khusrau I.
565 Death of Emperor Justinian.

AFRICA

c400 First towns south of the Sahara.
429 80,000 Vandals invade Roman province of North Africa.
442 Western Roman Empire forced to recognize the Vandal state of North Africa.
c450 Iron-working by the Nok people of West Africa.
455 Emperor Valentinian III assassinated. Vandal King Geiseric invades Italy and sacks Rome.
468 Eastern Roman Emperor Leo I's expedition against Vandals fails.
484 Huns kill Persian Sassanian Emperor.
c500 Arrival in southern Africa of Bantu people with ironworking and domesticated cattle.
531–79 Persian Sassanid Empire at its greatest under Khusrau I.
533 Eastern Roman Empire's successful expedition against the Vandals led by Justinian's general, Belisarius.

INDIA, FAR EAST

c480–500 Huns invade Gupta Empire in India and destroy it. Toramana is the first Hun king.
c500 Period of the Six Dynasties in China. Toba Wei empire established in northern China.
520 Mihirakula (Toramana's son) rules northern and central India despite some resistance.
c542 Mihirakula dies, driven into Kashmir.
552 Buddhist religion introduced into Japan from China.
550 Avars driven out of Mongolia.
581 China reunified under General Yang Chien who founds the Sui dynasty (lasts until 617).
c600 Hun invasions recede after counterattacks by as Persians and Turks.

The Huns, led by Attila, swept into Roman territory, destroying and killing as they went. However, in 451 the Romans defeated the Huns in battle, and when Attila died two years later the empire of the Huns collapsed. But the barbarian threat did not go away. The Visigoths controlled Spain, and the Vandals had set up their kingdom in North Africa. In 476 Odovacar, king of a group of German tribes that had settled in Italy, threw out the last Roman Emperor in the west, Romulus Augustulus.

The Eastern Roman Empire under Justinian

Until the early 6th century the Eastern Roman Empire had no influence on events in the west. But in 527 a new Emperor, Justinian, came to the throne. Supported by his determined wife Theodora, he soon established himself as a powerful ruler. Justinian's Eastern Roman Empire is also known as the Byzantine Empire. In 533 Justinian began to campaign against the 'barbarians', and within a few months his armies had won back North Africa.

By 554 he had reconquered southern Spain as well as the whole of Italy, Sicily and Sardinia. Under the Ostrogoth Theodoric, (see page 9) the capital of Italy had moved to Ravenna and it was from here that Justinian's general, Narses, ruled the west. But this rule did not last. After Justinian's death in 565, Italy was invaded once again – this time by the Lombards, another barbarian tribe from the east who had settled in what is now Hungary. Later, in the 7th century, Africa and then Spain were taken over by the Muslims (see page 23).

From about 570 the Byzantine Empire itself (see page 6) was attacked by the Avars, who lived north of the River Danube. It also came under threat from a revived Persian Empire, and a war that started between the two states in 561 lasted for 20 years.

AMERICAS, PACIFIC

c400 Easter Island and Hawaii islands (in the Pacific Ocean) settled by Polynesians.
c500 Hopewell peoples of North America in decline.
c500 Farming introduced into the forests of Brazil from the River Amazon area.
500 Thule hunters arrived in Alaska, spread across northern Arctic to Greenland.
600 Beginning of Mississippi temple mounds in North America.
600 Tiahuanaco, highest city and religious center in the Andes, has a population of about 35,000.
c600 City of Teotihuacan in Mesoamerica covers over 8 sq miles.
c600 Mayan civilization at its height. Development of calendars, astronomy, writing, architecture and arts. Mayans dominate Mesoamerica.

CLOVIS – KING OF THE FRANKS

Clovis began as a leader of those Franks who lived around the town of Tournai (now in Belgium). But by the time of his death in 511, he was recognized as king of all the Franks and had his capital in Paris. His conversion to Christianity in 507 won him support from the clergy. Here, Clovis is being crowned king, attended by his wife Clotilda, a princess from Burgundy who was already a Christian. Clovis's kingdom covered the countries now known as France, Belgium, the Netherlands, Luxembourg, Switzerland and Germany.

The spread of Christianity

Against the background of warfare between peoples over land, there was a rise in the influence of Christianity. Many of the peoples who were regarded by the Romans in Constantinople as 'barbarians' were in fact Christians, including Clovis, the king of the Franks (see page 11). In 631 the Emperor Justinian sent a monk called Julian to convert the people in Ethiopia to Christianity, and later he also went on to Nubia. But Roman Emperors wanted to rule both the State and the Church, and this led to a clash between the Emperor and the Pope, based in Rome, from the 5th century.

In the late 6th century Pope Gregory I established the Church in Rome as a powerful force. Although Christianity was now the official religion within the Roman world, it was not followed by everyone in Europe. Many 'pagan' religions survived or were introduced by new peoples. To convert these peoples to Christianity the Pope sent out missions, the best-known of which was led by Augustine (see right).

Augustine and his monks with Bertha, the king's wife

▼ ST AUGUSTINE IN BRITAIN

Pope Gregory I sent out monks from Rome as missionaries to spread the idea of the Roman Church – the Catholic Church. Missions went to Spain and to Gaul (now France), but probably the most famous was the one to Britain. Gregory sent a monk called Augustine, who was the Prior of St Andrew's monastery in Rome, together with 40 monks to convert the Angles in southern Britain. They arrived in 597, landing at the Isle of Thanet in Kent, where they met the king, Ethelbert, and his wife Bertha. She was already a Christian and persuaded her husband to support Augustine's mission. On Christmas Day in 597 Augustine is said to have converted 10,000 people. As a reward, Pope Gregory made him Archbishop of Canterbury, where he founded a monastery, and Primate of Britain (the chief bishop).

△ This monastery founded by St Augustine in 598 was dedicated to St Peter and St Paul and was a home for Benedictine monks. Originally there were three separate churches here. In the 11th century the monastery was reconstructed.

▶ COLLAPSE OF THE GUPTA EMPIRE

Northern India was governed by members of the Gupta Dynasty (family) from the 4th to the 6th centuries. The reign of this powerful dynasty began in about 335 with Chandra Gupta I, who called himself *maharajadhiraja* ('great king of kings'). The Guptas controlled a large area of north-east and west India from their capital at Pataliputra. Many other kings throughout India were forced to pay homage to them. A Chinese Buddhist pilgrim, who visited India at the beginning of the 5th century, described the country as a happy one. It was a great age for Indian art and culture. But by the middle of the century this civilized empire was threatened by Huns from central Asia who then invaded and seized control of north-west India.

An Indian Buddhist temple

By the year 600, the missionaries sent to Gaul had set up over 200 monasteries there (see page 34). But there was trouble closer to home from the Lombards, who had invaded Italy in 568. Pope Gregory complained that they had burned down churches and devastated the land. By the 7th century the Lombards occupied much of Italy, although some parts, including the area around Rome, still belonged to the Roman Empire.

▼ TEOTIHUACAN

By the year 500 there were probably 200,000 people living in the city of Teotihuacan in Mesoamerica. The city had been occupied from about AD 150. Its most impressive monument was the Pyramid of the Sun, which rises over 200ft above the ruins of the vast city which occupied more than 8 sq miles. People journeyed to Teotihuacan from all over Mesoamerica to worship their gods because they thought that it was here that the Sun and the Moon were born. The city's temples also contain carvings of other gods, such as Quetzalcoatl, the Feathered Serpent.

Teotihuacan and the Pyramid of the Sun

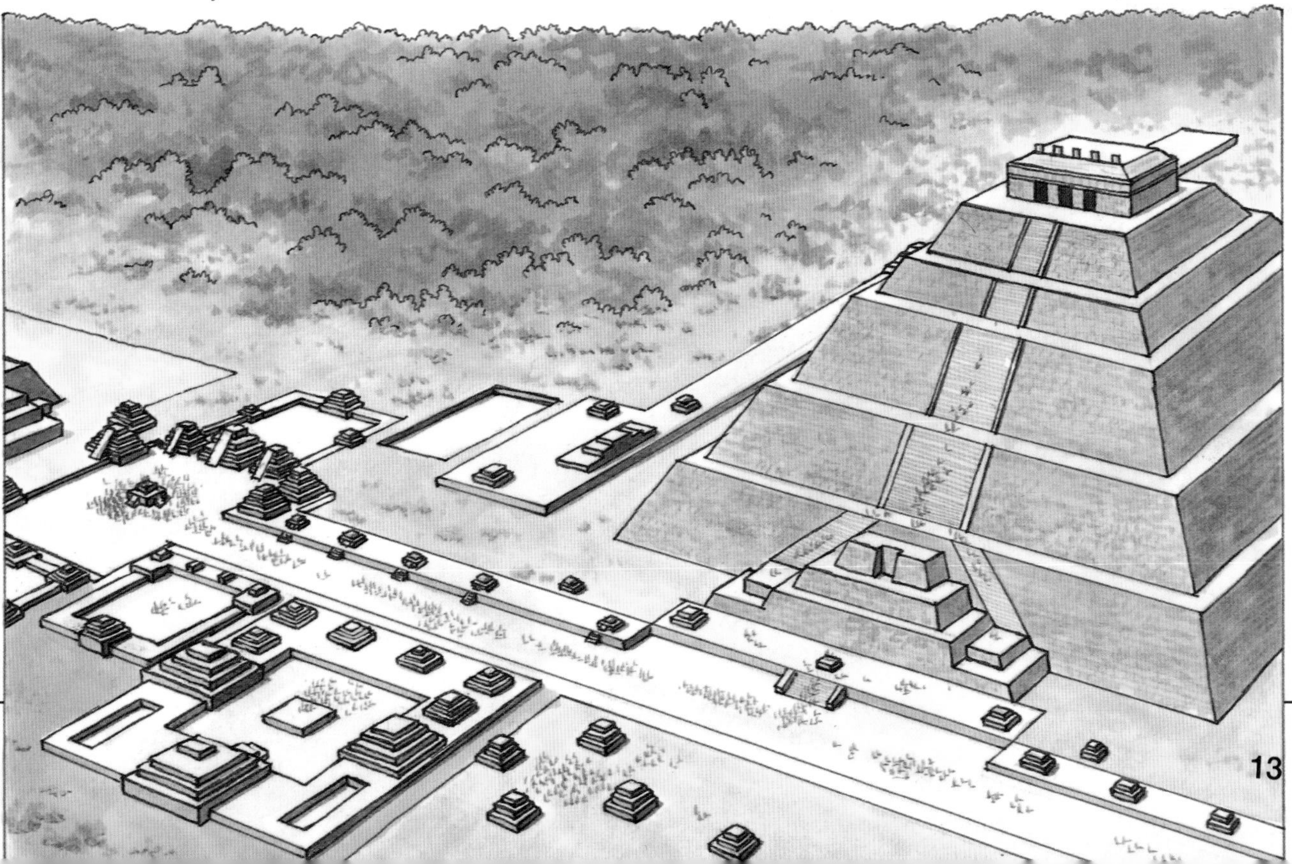

BUDDHISM

Buddhism is a religion that was begun by Siddhartha Gautama Buddha around 530 BC. It is still practiced today by millions of people all over the world. Buddhists believe that each person should do good works, should be disciplined throughout his or her life and should spend time in meditation.

Siddhartha Gautama's father was the ruler of the Sakya tribe in northern India during the Mauryan Empire. When he was 29, Gautama received four signs which led him to leave his home and his family for six years in search of the 'true wisdom'. After a final night of meditation, he reached a state he called 'enlightenment' and became the *Buddha*, meaning 'The Enlightened One'.

The spread of Buddhism

After the Buddha's death in 483 BC, some of his followers formed an order of Buddhist monks to spread the religion. It became the main religion of the Mauryan Empire and from there it spread southwards and northwards. Accordingly, two main branches of Buddhism developed. The first, *theravada*, meaning teachings of the elders, by the 7th century had spread to Srī Lanka, Thailand, Cambodia and Java. The second branch, *mahayana*, or 'great message', reached Tibet, China, Korea and Japan by about the same time. Between 450 and 700, followers of the Buddha built monuments and monasteries and made inscriptions on special pillars to spread the Buddha's beliefs.

BUDDHISM

BC
566 Siddhartha Gautama born in northern India.
537 Gautama receives four signs and begins his search.
531 He reaches the state of Enlightenment, called Nirvana, and becomes the Buddha.
486 Buddha dies after spending his life preaching that the middle way, or *Dhamma*, between extremes is the right way for people to live.
270–232 Emperor Asoka rules the Mauryan Empire – Buddhism spreads through India.

Chinese statue of the Buddha

AD
1st-2nd centuries Buddhism spreads to southern and north-western India and Mongolia.
65 First reference to Buddhism in China made by Emperor Han Ming-ti.
500 Buddhism reaches all provinces of China.
552 Buddhism introduced into Japan from China.
594 Japan adopts Buddhism as official religion.
624 Buddhism becomes official religion of China.
645 Buddhism introduced into Tibet. First Buddhist temple built there in **651**.
7th century Buddhism introduced into Java from India and Sri Lanka. Temple at Borobudur, Java, built **c800**.
1185 Zen Buddhist order founded in Japan (from the word *zenna* meaning 'quiet mind concentration'.

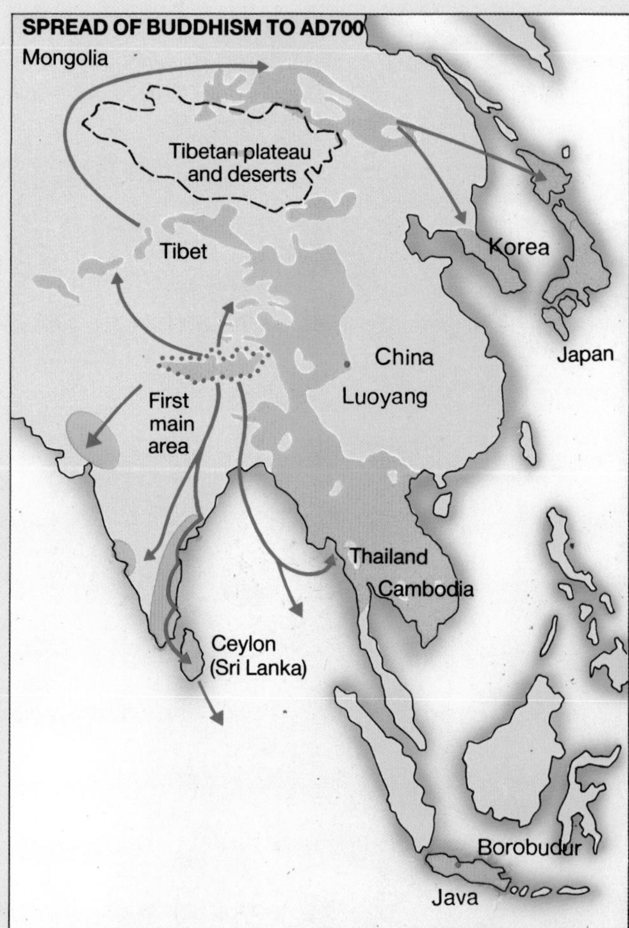

◁ *Inset* The Buddha was depicted as a mother-figure. This statue is from cave-temples near Luoyang in China dating to the late 7th century.

◁ A reclining Buddha from the 12th century, found at Polonnaruwa, the capital of Sri Lanka, an island to which Buddhist monks traveled.

▽ A Buddhist *stupa*, with a square base and central mound, at Borobudur in Java.

OLD EMPIRES, NEW FORCES

Both in the West and the Far East the old civilizations experienced upheaval from the 7th century. In the Near East, a new force – Islam – soon built its own civilization and swept others aside. Meanwhile, nomadic tribes from the Russian steppes expanded across Europe and reached China.

The rise of Islam

In Europe and the Near East the rise of Islam (see pages 22-3) was the most important development of the period. In the 7th century the land of Arabia lay outside the territory of the Byzantine Empire. Islam, the religion of the prophet Muhammad, appealed to the poor nomads and townspeople of Arabia. Islam's followers, called Muslims, were Arab warriors who believed that if they died in battle they would go straight to heaven.

Arab armies set off in all directions to conquer new lands and to threaten established empires. In the 7th century the Byzantine Empire was at war with the Persians. By 750 the Arabs had themselves defeated the Persians and occupied Iraq. They also marched into India, defeated a Chinese army, seized the whole of North Africa and Spain and captured Syria from the Byzantines.

The 7th-century town of Cahokia

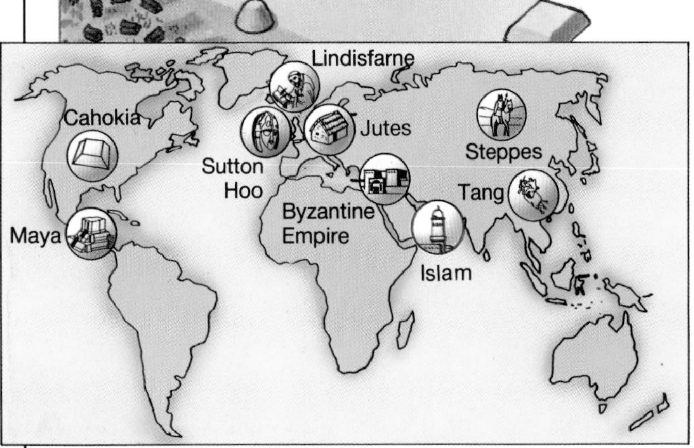

△ The new major force in the world at this time was Islam, which spread quickly from Arabia and threatened Europe. In the Americas the first towns appeared in the north, often with monumental buildings.

Ⓐ CAHOKIA, MISSISSIPPI

Around 600 the first towns and cities developed in North America in the central part of the Mississippi River valley. One of these was Cahokia, near the modern city of St. Louis. By about 1200 there were probably 10,000 people living there – and, very likely, Cahokia was the place that governed the other 16 towns of the surrounding region. Many people were farmers who lived in small villages around the main towns, growing crops such as corn, beans, squash, nuts and sunflowers. They also hunted and fished. The towns had large open squares surrounded by tall flat-topped mounds. Some of the mounds were used for the burial of the dead, and the wooden buildings on top of the mounds were probably temples. The wooden wall around the center of the city was put up in about 1200.

Mounted Chinese hunters

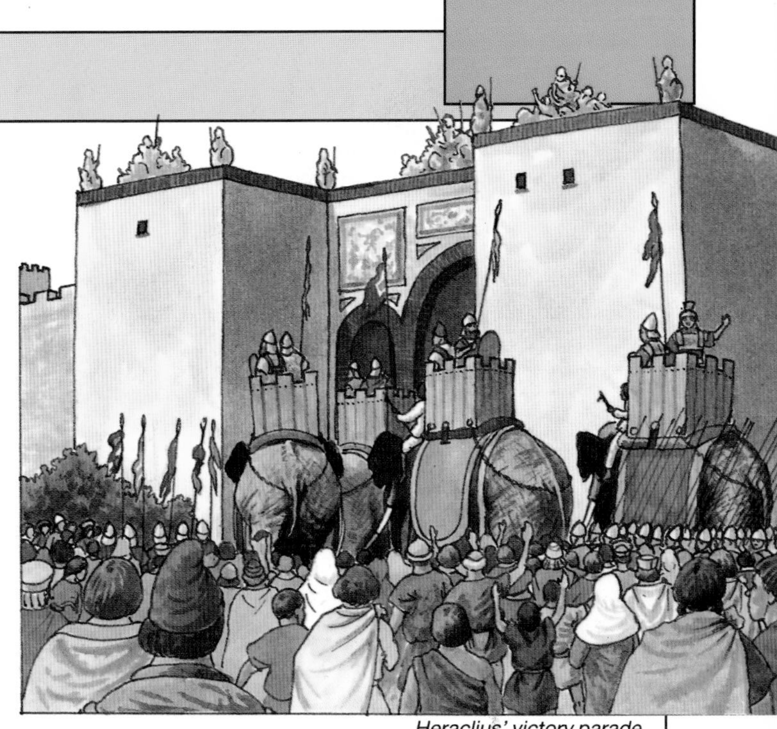

Heraclius' victory parade

Ⓐ TANG DYNASTY, CHINA

Much of the evidence we have for the Tang Dynasty in China, which began in 618, comes from the capital Chang'an. There, excavations of the city and the royal tombs have shown a very cultured society with the most beautiful pottery, embroidered silk and figurines – especially of horses with their riders. Other popular figurines were camels laden with goods. The tombs had wall paintings in them showing life for the nobles and the rich of the period. This illustration is taken from the tomb of Li Shou, who died at Sanyuan in 630. A favorite pastime was hunting on horseback with bows and arrows. The prey included foxes, hares, deer and wild boar.

Ⓐ THE BYZANTINE EMPIRE

When the Emperor Heraclius came to the throne in 610 the Byzantine Empire was under threat from the Persians. Less than 20 years later he led a victory parade through the capital, Constantinople, carrying with him the spoils of his Persian campaign. At the head of the parade on 14 September 628 was the True Cross, which Christians believed was the cross on which Christ was crucified. It had been recaptured from the Persians, who had taken it from Jerusalem and then destroyed the city. Emperor Heraclius marched with four elephants (never seen before in Constantinople) through the Golden Gate – a ceremonial arch built by Emperor Theodosius the Great in 390.

600–640

606 First written examination in Chinese civil service.
610 Byzantine Empire begins with reign of Emperor Heraclius.
613 Muhammad begins preaching in Mecca.
613 Jerusalem falls to the Persians.
618 Tang Dynasty begins in China.
624 Buddhism becomes official religion of China.
625 Sutton Hoo ship burial, England.
630 Muslims control Arabia from Mecca.
632 The Prophet Muhammad dies.
636 Muslims control Syria after defeating Byzantine army.

640–750

641 Muslims capture Alexandria in Egypt. Emperor Heraclius dies.
664 Synod of Whitby establishes Roman Church practices in England.
697 Muslims in control of North Africa.
700 Anasazi people in American South-west build large settlements.
711 Muslims occupy Spain.
715 Muslims conquer Sind in India.
732 Franks defeat Muslims and drive them out of France.
751 Muslims defeat a Chinese army in central Asia.

The Byzantine Empire

The reign of the Emperor Heraclius, beginning in 610, was the start of the true Byzantine Empire. He drew together all that really remained of the old Greek and Roman civilizations in his capital at Constantinople. His people were Greek-speaking and Christian. Heraclius also finally put paid to the threat from Persia. The decisive defeat of the Persians at Nineveh in 626 led to the collapse of the Persian Empire.

Yet, even during Heraclius' reign, the power of the Byzantines was being seriously challenged. The Muslims were the most serious threat. Arab armies besieged the capital Constantinople in 674–8 and again in 717–18, while to the north the Bulgars advanced into what had been Greece. Eventually, in the 9th and 10th centuries the Muslims and the Bulgars were beaten back, but by then Byzantine power was nearly at an end (see page 32).

The threat from the north

Having survived the threat from nomadic peoples such as the Huns and the Goths, the Mediterranean world now faced a new wave of invasions by people from the steppes of Russia. The steppes stretched from eastern Europe to Asia. The nomadic tribes gradually moved west across the grassy steppe lands, pushing out the inhabitants and threatening the territory of established civilizations. Eventually they built their own states – Turks in Turkey, Magyars in Hungary, and Bulgars (themselves Huns), who mixed with Slavs and founded Bulgaria.

▲ THE TRIBES OF THE STEPPES

Throughout southern Russia there are huge areas of open grassland known as the steppes. From there, waves of warriors on horseback swept across eastern, and then western, Europe. The steppe peoples lived in tribes known as hordes. The leader of a horde was called a khan. During the 6th and 7th centuries a number of these peoples began to make their homes in villages and to farm the land. Evidence from their settlements, such as tools, stone reliefs and the silver figurines above, showed that they kept sheep, goats, pigs and chickens.

WESTERN EUROPE

625 Sutton Hoo ship burial. Death of Raedwald, High King of Britain.
634 Christianity carried to Northumbria, England.
653 East Anglia, England, becomes Christian.
664 Synod of Whitby, called by Oswy, King of Northumbria, establishes that the Church in England follows the Roman Church of the Pope.
687 Pepin II defeats his rivals in battle and becomes sole ruler of the Franks.
698 Lindisfarne Gospels are the first psalms produced in the language of the Anglo-Saxons.
711 Muslims occupy Spain.
732 Charles Martel, King of the Franks, defeats the Muslims at Poitiers. Muslims driven out of France.
751 Pepin III founds the Carolingian Dynasty in France.

E. ROMAN EMPIRE

610 Heraclius becomes Eastern Roman Emperor. Empire now known as the Byzantine Empire.
613 Jerusalem, the Holy City, falls to the Persians.
619 Persians threaten Constantinople.
626 Heraclius defeats the Persians at Nineveh. Persian Empire collapses.
636 Byzantine army defeated by Muslims at Yarmuk in Syria.
641 Muslims invade Egypt and capture Alexandria.
641 Heraclius dies.
674–8 Constantinople besieged by Muslim armies.
680 Bulgars invade the Balkan territory of the Byzantine Empire.
697 Byzantine rule in North Africa taken over by Muslims.
717–18 Constantinople besieged by Muslims.
717 Beginning of struggle in Byzantium over the use of religious images – icons – which opponents say leads to idolatry.

AFRICA, INDIA

600 Power of the Pallava peoples established in southern India under the ruler Mahendra-varman I. Rock-cut temples at Mahabalipuram built during his reign.
600 Kingdom of Ghana, first state in West Africa, founded.
618 Persians conquer Egypt.
698 Arabs conquer Carthage on North African coast and convert the African people to Islam.
700 Arabs begin trading with African cities south of the Sahara Desert.
711 Muslims in control of North Africa and Spain.
715 Muslims conquer Sind in north-east India.
736 Founding of the city of Dhillika, the first city of Delhi.
740 Pallava power destroyed by the Chalukya people in southern India.
c750 City of Jenne-Jeno in West Africa has city wall of bricks completed.

THE FAR EAST

580–604 Emperor Weng rules the Sui Dynasty.
605–10 Millions of laborers dig Imperial canal to join the Yangtze and Huanh Ho rivers.
606 First written examination for Chinese civil service entrants.
607 Tibet becomes unified as a state.
618–907 The Tang Dynasty in China.
624 Buddhism becomes China's religion.
637–49 Under the Emperor T'ai Tsung the Tang Dynasty reaches its height.
645 Buddhist religion reaches Tibet.
650 Tibet begins to expand.
650 Polynesian islands settled except New Zealand.
695 Mongol people invade northern China.
710 Beginning of the Nara period in Japan.
751 Muslim armies defeat the Chinese at the Battle of the River Talas.

Cities and civilizations in the Americas

For centuries there had been advanced civilizations in America – in the narrow coastal lands called Mesoamerica and in the Andes region. In Mesoamerica the greatest of these civilizations – the Maya – arose. These people had been building towns from 300 BC but had been influenced by other peoples, notably the Olmecs. Now their civilization began to flourish in its own right.

▶ TIKAL, MAYA CITY

By the 8th century about 50,000 people lived in the city of Tikal, now in modern Guatemala, South America. Like other cities of the advanced Mayan civilization, Tikal was full of the most impressive buildings – plazas (open squares) surrounded with temple pyramids and temple palaces. Each of the cities of the Maya were independent, often fighting with their neighbors and taking prisoners for human sacrifice. Tikal was the largest Mayan city, which controlled the area around it, and was the headquarters of a paramount chief who ruled the region.

Mayans ascending a temple pyramid

THE AMERICAS

300–800 Golden age of Mayan civilization. Development of calendars, astronomy, writing, architecture and art. Mayans dominate Mesoamerica.
600–800 Towns and cities built along river valleys in North America. Very large populations, temple mounds in city centers.
615 Pacal becomes ruler of the Mayan city of Palenque at the age of 12, and city becomes very powerful.
650–750 Decline of city of Teotihuacan. Burned down but not abandoned.
700 Mayan city of Tikal rebuilt with five temple pyramids. Population now about 50,000.
700 Anasazi people in American South-west begin to build large settlements.

▶ JUTE VILLAGE

Various peoples – Angles, Saxons, Jutes and Frisians – lived in Scandinavia and Holland in the 7th and 8th centuries. This village was at a place now known as Sejlflod in northern Denmark. There were about five farms here – with some 50 people altogether. They grew mostly barley, but also wheat, oats and rye. They kept animals, mostly cattle and sheep, but they also reared pigs, ducks and geese. The people of Sejlflod made good use of their environment. They hunted wild boar, deer and hares, they fished and they collected berries and nuts.

SUTTON HOO SHIP BURIAL

A spectacular discovery was made in 1939 in the East Anglian region of England. The remains of an Anglo-Saxon warship were excavated under a burial mound. Archaeologists believe that the body, which had been buried inside the ship in about 625, was that of Raedwald, an East Anglian king who was proclaimed *Bretwalda*, or High King of Britain. Raedwald's body was surrounded by a large number of finely-made objects, including weapons, bowls and a purse for money.

Ship buried at Sutton Hoo

The period from AD 300 to about 800 was the 'golden age' of the Mayan peoples, as they organized themselves into independent states. These states were constantly at war with each other – not to gain more territory but to take prisoners for sacrifices to their gods. But in other respects the Maya were advanced for their time. They developed two types of calendars, they wrote in special pictures called 'glyphs' and their artists produced fine carvings and statues.

In North America the first real towns and cities were being built. Around the River Mississippi and other rivers such as the Alabama and the Arkansas, rich civilizations were growing up. These people were farmers and hunters who settled in huge numbers and lived together in large communities.

China and South-East Asia

Much of South-East Asia was dominated by the powerful Tang Dynasty of China, which began in 618. The Tang Dynasty had taken over China after years of rebellions and established a state that was controlled from the center. Then the Tang armies began to move beyond the borders of China and to seize control of or dominate other peoples' lands – Japan to the north-east, and westward into Tibet and beyond as far as the River Oxus and Persia. Throughout these regions China set up and maintained trading links, especially along the old Silk Road.

China's cultural influence on its neighbors was also strong. The Chinese written language and system of government were adopted by both Korea and Japan. Japan was ruled from the capital Nara, a city of 200,000 people that was founded in 710 and modelled on the Chinese capital Chang'an. Korea, in about AD 538, and then Japan, also adopted the Buddhist religion from China. But despite its power and influence, China too, like the old civilizations in the west, was threatened by invasions from nomadic tribes who lived on the Russian steppes.

△ This manuscript of the Gospels was written and illuminated at Lichfield monastery, England.

▷ Monks wrote out copies of the Gospels and other works by hand and illuminated them.

▲▶ CHRISTIAN ART

The 7th to 9th centuries were a period of great reorganization in the Christian Church in western Europe. This was also a time of missions to the 'unbelieving gentiles', as Pope Gregory II said in 719. By the late 7th century, England had been converted to Christianity, and a number of missions by Anglo-Saxon Christians were sent from England to mainland Europe. The Christian religion was expressed in the art that people produced – in illuminated manuscripts, carved crosses and jeweled crucifixes. The monks from their monasteries created some outstanding works of art. The symbols of Christianity were often mixed with those from other cultures and other countries.

△ The tombstone of Gilbert, Bishop of Paris, has carving typical of the 7th century.

▷ Carved stone crosses were a common sight in the early Christian period. This is one of fifty made before 800 in Ireland, at Castledermot.

THE RISE OF ISLAM

In 570 a boy called Muhammad (the name means 'worthy of praise') was born in the tribe of the Quraysh in Mecca. When both his parents died, he was brought up by his grandfather who also lived there. The city of Mecca was already a holy place where pagan idols were worshipped. Muhammad travelled with his merchant uncle throughout Arabia on camel trains, before getting married at the age of 25.

The prophet Muhammad

In 610 he began to have messages from God. Muhammad preached that there was only one true God, and his religion was called Islam, which means 'submitting to God'. He and the followers of the new religion were called Muslims. They upset the powerful merchants of Mecca, who were worried that their wealth would disappear if people did not visit the holy shrine in Mecca.

Muhammad was forced to flee Mecca and in 622 he set up his Muslim community in the city of Medina to the north.

By 624 the Muslims in Medina were strong enough to defeat an army from Mecca at Badr. They then set about defeating any tribes who opposed their new religion. By the time of the Prophet Muhammad's death in 632, nearly all of Arabia had been converted to Islam.

ISLAM

570 Muhammad born in Mecca.
576 Muhammad's mother dies. He is brought up by his grandfather in Mecca.
610 Muhammad begins to have messages from God.
613 In Mecca Muhammad begins preaching.
622 He moves to Medina as head of a community of Muslims.
630 Most of Arabia converted to Islam.
632 Muhammad dies.
636 Muslim army defeats Byzantine forces and takes control of Syria.
643 Muslims overcome Persian Empire.
698 Muslims capture Carthage in North Africa.
711 Muslims occupy Spain.
715 Muslim armies conquer Sind in north-west India.
732 Muslim defeat by the Franks at Poitiers.
751 Muslim victory over a Chinese army at the Battle of the River Talas.

Plan of a mosque

△▷ Muslim towns (right) were busy with bustling markets. All towns had special places for worship and study called mosques, where Muslims could pray. Each mosque (above) has a *mihrab*, indicating the direction of Mecca which Muslims kneel to face when at prayer, and a minaret, from where people are called to prayer.

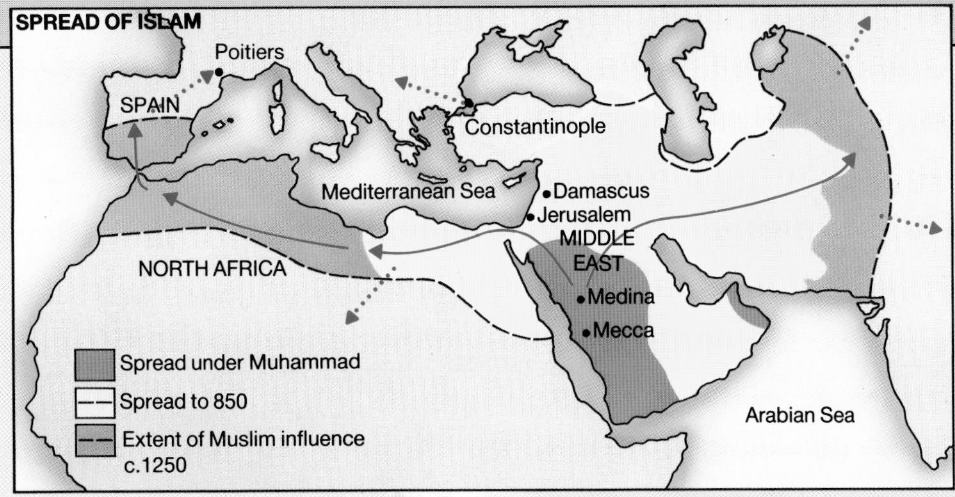

◁ The Islamic Empire in about 750. A century after the death of the Prophet Muhammad, the Arab Muslims had extended their empire beyond Arabia. Two areas were particularly important – west to Egypt and North Africa and then into Spain, and east to Iraq, India and China.

△ The holiest book for the followers of Islam was, and still is, the Quran. This book contains the messages that Muhammad received from God. The hand-written and hand-painted books were often very elaborate.

NEW KINGDOMS

In many parts of the world people were searching for new lands, sometimes to trade with foreign peoples, sometimes to find a place to settle. People looking for new homes were almost always unwelcome, and like the Vikings (see page 28) they were often feared. Across the world in Mesoamerica great changes were taking place. We do not know why, but by about 900 the Mayan civilization in the lowlands had collapsed.

Raiders in longships

The Vikings – raiders from Scandinavia – came in longships which carried up to 200 trained and ferocious warriors. Vikings from Denmark were the first to move, and in the 9th century they settled in other parts of Europe. By 911 the Viking leader Rollo was made Duke of Normandy ('the land of the Northerners') by the Franks.

Britain – Anglo-Saxon and Viking

Angles and Saxons had come to Britain from Germany during the Roman period. In the 8th century they divided the country into kingdoms, such as Offa's kingdom of Mercia (see below). By the late 9th century Danish Vikings had taken over much of Britain, establishing settlements such as the busy town of *Jorvik*, which had once been the Anglo-Saxon capital of Northumbria, called *Eoforwic*. By the middle of the 10th century the situation had reversed, with English kings in control.

▼ ANGLO-SAXON KINGDOMS

Britain in the 8th century was divided into a number of small kingdoms. From 757 the central kingdom, called Mercia, was ruled by King Offa, who was known as *Bretwalda*, meaning 'High King of Britain'. Offa's kingdom eventually became very large, taking in East Anglia and Kent and threatening the kingdom of Wessex. The lands ruled by King Offa were themselves threatened by raids from Welsh tribes, and so by 790 Offa had built a huge dyke – a defensive wall of earth and wood – to protect Mercia. Offa's Dyke was about 150 miles long, stretching from coast to coast. The building was done in sections by gangs of men from all over Mercia as a form of military service.

▽ King Offa is shown on this coin – a silver penny. He reorganized the coinage in use throughout Mercia during his reign.

Building the dyke around Offa's kingdom

African traders on the River Niger

THE MAGYARS

In the late 9th century, nomadic tribes came on horseback from the Russian steppes into what is now Hungary. These were the Magyars. They raided other peoples' territory, looking for booty and slaves, and reached Italy, Germany and even as far as France. The people around them were forced to build castles for defense and to organize their farms around these fortifications. The Magyars were finally defeated in 955 by the German King Otto I, and those who had led the raids were executed. Two of their other chiefs were baptized into Christianity at Constantinople. The statue of Magyar chiefs (above) is in Budapest.

TRANS-SAHARA ROUTES

From the 5th century a number of rich trading towns grew up in West Africa along the River Niger. By the 8th century other centers, such as Ife in Nigeria, were also trading goods to the north. The Arabs encouraged long-distance trade in goods across the Sahara Desert.

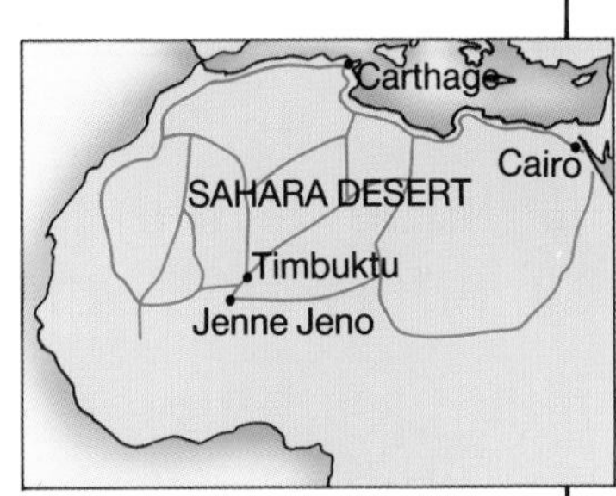

△ Desert trade routes for slaves, ivory and gold.

750–800

750 Muslims control all sea-trade between Red Sea and China.
750 City of Teotihuacan destroyed by fire.
751 Pepin III founds the Carolingian Dynasty of the Franks.
751 Chinese defeated by Muslims at River Talas.
762 Capital of Muslim Empire moved to Baghdad.
771 Charlemagne proclaimed King of the Franks.
774 Charlemagne becomes King of Italy.
793 First Viking raid on Britain at Lindisfarne.
795 Franks create marches (frontier zones) in Spain and Pannonia.
800 Towns develop in North America. Bow and arrow first used.
800 West African kingdoms established.

800–950

800 Charlemagne crowned Holy Roman Emperor by the Pope.
830 Kingdom of Moravia established by the Slavs.
844 Viking raids on Spain and Portugal.
860 Viking settlers reach Iceland.
862 Christian missions to Moravia by St Cyril and St Methodius.
866 Conversion of Russia to Christianity begins.
878 King Alfred the Great defeats the Vikings.
885 Paris besieged by the Vikings.
900 Anasazi farmers in North America build cliff houses.
907 Civil wars in China. Mongol expansion into northern China.
911 Rollo the Viking is made Duke of Normandy.
950 Toltec city of Tula founded in Mesoamerica.

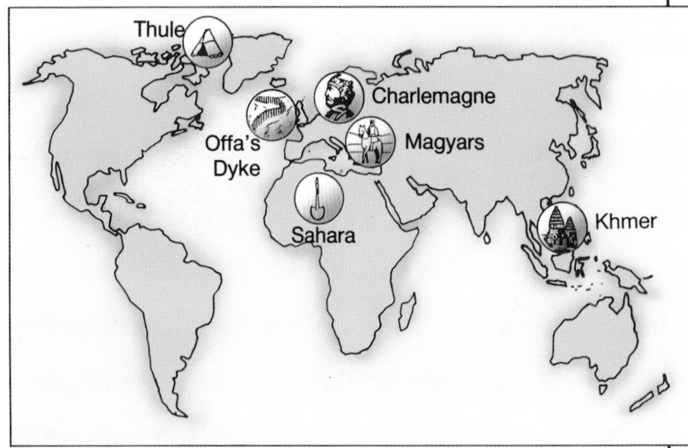

△ Two opposing developments changed the way people lived. While some peoples built defensive boundaries on their lands – the dyke of King Offa, for example – many others were on the move, looking for new lands to settle. They included the Vikings and the people of the Mediterranean and Near East who began to penetrate Africa.

Establishing the Christian religion

Despite the threats from Muslim armies, Christianity was on the increase. The Franks, who were Christian, extended their empire under their Emperor Charlemagne (see opposite). They defeated the Saxons and others in Germany and converted them to Christianity. They also created protected frontier lands, called marches, as buffer zones between themselves and their enemies.

The Vikings, who travelled and settled in Europe at a time when it was almost entirely Christian, became Christians themselves – both abroad and in their own homelands.

Meanwhile an eastern form of the Christian religion, established in Constantinople, was also spreading. Two missionaries who became famous, St Cyril and St Methodius, brought Christianity to Moravia (modern Czechoslovakia) in the early 9th century, and by 866 it was beginning to spread into Russia. Nomadic tribes who adopted the Christian religion became more settled.

▲ CHARLEMAGNE

Charlemagne – center left, in red on horseback.

By 768 the empire of the Franks stretched from the Netherlands to the borders of Spain, and from Brittany to Bohemia. A royal prince, Charles, took over this huge empire in 771 and reigned as emperor for over 45 years. He became known as Charlemagne, from the Latin *Carolus Magnus*, which means Charles the Great. Charlemagne increased the size of the empire by fighting about 60 military campaigns. He conquered the Saxons and invaded Italy and Bavaria. His exploits were recognized by the Pope in Rome who crowned him Emperor of the West – the Holy Roman Empire.

▶ THULE HUNTERS

The Thule people hunted and fished along the coast of Alaska from about 500. They used dog sledges and boats called kayaks and invented new sorts of bows and harpoons. In summer they camped in tents while hunting the seal and walrus and fishing for whales. In winter they built better houses to protect them from the Arctic weather. These houses were dug into the ground with tunnel entrances to trap the warm air inside. By about 1000 the Thule people had moved east to conquer other peoples' territory.

Seal hunters of Alaska

WESTERN EUROPE

751 Pepin III becomes King of the Franks and founds the Carolingian Dynasty.
771 One of Pepin's sons becomes sole ruler of the Franks and is known as Charlemagne.
772–804 Saxon defeats by the Franks.
773–4 Charlemagne conquers Lombardy, becomes King of Italy.
795 Franks create marches (frontier zones) in Spain and Pannonia.
793 First recorded Viking raid on England at Lindisfarne.
800 Charlemagne crowned on Christmas Day by the Pope as Emperor of the Holy Roman Empire.
814 Charlemagne dies.
843 Holy Roman Empire divided into three parts.
878 Danelaw in England to control Viking settlers.
911 Rollo the Viking made Duke of Normandy.

The Sahara and beyond

The Muslims had already established themselves as a major world power and were occupying new territories just as the Vikings and Franks had done. They were also great travellers and merchants. Because of trade with the Arabs in slaves and in goods such as ivory, gold and ebony, West African towns such as Ife and Jenne-Jeno (see page 30) were known to the people who lived in Europe around the Mediterranean.

▶ KHMER STATE: ANGKOR

The rulers of the Khmer kingdom (now Cambodia and Thailand) developed a state which became wealthy through the production of rice. With this wealth the Khmer kings, who thought of themselves as gods, ordered the building of hundreds of elaborate, highly decorated temples. Angkor, which was the capital state, and other Khmer cities were full of temples, palaces, irrigation canals, and reservoirs called *baray*, used for religious rituals. The first *baray* to be built at Angkor in 889 measured about 1 mile by 4 miles. The famous Angkor Wat temple was not built until the early 12th century.

A Khmer temple

EASTERN EUROPE

726–843 Icons prohibited in Byzantine churches.
751 Fall of Ravenna. Byzantine rule ends in Italy.
787 Council of Nicaea restores use of icons.
812 Bulgarians defeat Byzantines in Battle of Adrianople.
830 Kingdom of Moravia established by the Slavs.
862 Mission to Moravia by St Cyril and St Methodius to convert people to Christianity.
862 Rurik the Viking founds Novgorod in Russia.
863 Cyril develops the Cyrillic alphabet.
865 Khan Boris of Bulgaria christened.
866 Beginning of conversion of Russia to Byzantine Christianity.
867 Basil I becomes Byzantine Emperor.
889 Magyars invade Hungary and establish a state there.

MIDDLE EAST

750 Muslims control all trade by sea between the Red Sea and China.
750 End of rule of Muslim world by the Omayyad Dynasty.
750 Rule by the Abbasid Caliphs who extend Muslim Empire.
754 al-Mansur succeeds as the Caliph of the Abbasid Dynasty.
762 Capital of Muslim Empire moved to Baghdad. Leadership passes to Persians.
786–809 Reign of Caliph Harun al-Rashid (famous from the *Thousand and One Nights* stories). Muslim Empire begins to break up.
788 Idrisid Dynasty founded in Morocco.
800 West African kingdoms established.
801 Aghlabids Dynasty at Kairwan in North Africa.
909 Fatamid Dynasty takes over Arab kingdoms in North Africa.

THE FAR EAST

618–907 Tang Dynasty in China.
751 Muslim armies defeat the Chinese at the Battle of the River Talas.
790 Conquest of west of China by the Tufan kingdom.
794 Establishment of the Heian period in Japan. Aristocracy of officials and warriors. Capital moves to Kyoto.
844 Buddhists persecuted in China.
868 World's first printed book, *The Diamond Sutra*, in China.
907–960 Civil wars in China. Period of the Five Dynasties.
907 Mongol expansion into Inner Mongolia and northern China.
918 State of Koryo established in Korea.
939 Vietnam becomes independent of China.
960 Sung Dynasty unites central and southern China.

THE AMERICAS

750 City of Teotihuacan destroyed by fire.
800-900 Mayan civilization in decline. Many cities abandoned.
800 Towns in central North America develop. Bow and arrow first used (replacing spear and dart) to make hunting easier.
800 Farming villages built in eastern plains of North America.
800 Mogollon people in New Mexico and eastern Arizona establish farming villages.
800 Dorset Inuit people in Greenland and north-east Canada.
900 Anasazi farmers begin building pueblos – buildings in cliffs.
900 Hohokam farmers in American South-west build irrigation canals.
947 Birth of Quetzalcoatl, considered a god by the Aztecs.
950 Toltec city of Tula founded.

THE VIKINGS

The name Vikings comes from the word *víkingr* in the Old Norse language. The word meant a pirate or raider but was used to describe all those people who lived in what is now Norway, Sweden and Denmark. The Vikings were great traders, reaching as far as Constantinople and North America.

Not all the Vikings lived up to their fierce reputation. Most were farmers who planted a variety of crops – wheat, oats, barley and vegetables – and kept animals such as cattle, sheep, pigs and chickens. Viking people also enjoyed hunting and fishing. Their artists and craft workers produced beautiful objects in metalwork, bone and stone.

▽ Part of the vast collection of Viking silver known as the Cuerdale hoard. It dates to the early 10th century and was found near the River Ribble in England. The Cuerdale hoard is the largest Viking hoard found in northern or western Europe.

Both men and women dressed in brightly colored clothing with decoration and jewelery. Women often wore headscarves and an ankle-length dress. Men wore a tunic or shirt over a pair of woollen trousers.

Seafaring Vikings

The Vikings were great shipbuilders and fine sailors. In the 8th century they set sail from Scandinavia in their long ships. Some went north and west to find new homes and build farms in places like Greenland and North America. Others went looking for rich plunder and slaves. Some settled in Britain and Ireland and built towns.

THE VIKINGS

c700 Viking expeditions to Shetland Islands.
c790 Viking raids on Europe.
793 First raid on Britain. Lindisfarne sacked.
832 The Vikings reach Ireland.
836 Dublin established as a Viking town.
844 Raids on Spain and Portugal.
860 Viking settlers arrive in Iceland.
862 Novgorod, Russia, founded by Rurik the Viking.
866 Viking army marches from East Anglia, England to York, where the capital Jorvik is set up.
878 King Alfred the Great of England defeats the Vikings. Danelaw established, allowing Vikings to live in only one area.
882 Vikings from Sweden form a state based at Kiev.
885 Paris besieged by the Vikings.

▷ A stone erected by King Harald 'Bluetooth' of Denmark. On the other side it shows the Crucifixion.

VIKING TRADE AND PLUNDER ROUTES TO 1000

◁ By 1000 the Vikings had conquered new lands and established distant trading links (above). The Danish Viking town of Hedeby, which was founded in 808 as a trading town with its own harbor, might have looked like this (left). Its workshops made fine objects from bone and metal for export. Hedeby was destroyed by Norwegian Vikings in 1050.

EMPIRE BUILDING

In Mesoamerica the people that emerged as the strongest and most advanced were the Toltecs. They were a mixture of two nomadic tribes – one from the Tolteca-Chichimeca Desert and the other the Nonoalca people from the coast of the Gulf of Mexico. The Toltecs founded cities in the Valley of Mexico, with their capital city at Tula. Away from their large, well-planned cities however, the Toltecs were ferocious and warlike. They conquered the area around the Gulf of Mexico, seizing food to feed their armies.

In about 987, worship of the god of the region, Quetzalcoatl, was banned in Tula, but was probably carried on in Chichen Itza (see page 31). The Toltecs' new god was Tezcatoipoca – the god of life and death – and, like other civilizations of Mesoamerica, worship by the Toltecs involved human sacrifice.

American cliff-dwellers

On the North American continent new civilizations were emerging. In the southwest, in the area that is today Utah, Colorado, New Mexico and Arizona, the Anasazi people built great settlements such as Mesa Verde (see Anasazi cliff dwellers, page 35). The largest of these, Pueblo Bonito in the Chaco Canyon of New Mexico, had a population of about 1,200. The Anasazi were farmers, who grew corn, squash and beans and kept turkeys. They also hunted deer, rats and squirrel for food. Their settlements were fortified against attack, but we do not know who they were afraid of. The people of Mesa Verde protected their houses and religious rooms by building into the cliffs. Pueblo Bonito was built in the shape of a letter D with an outer wall four stories high.

▽ In Africa, kingdoms were developing and establishing links with one another. Meanwhile, in northern Europe, a new force, the Normans, were emerging, while the Toltecs controlled Mesoamerica.

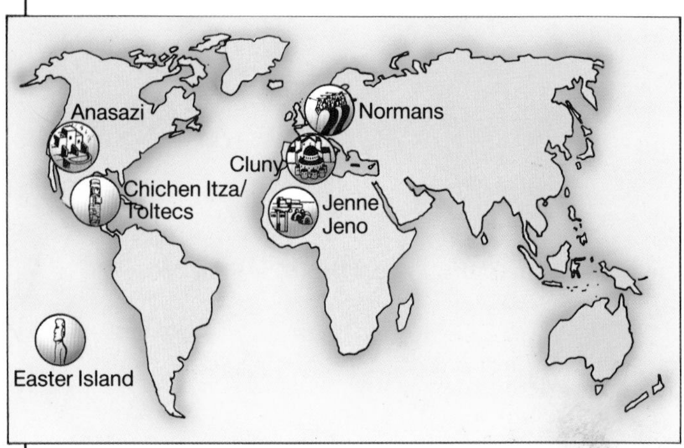

JENNE-JENO – A CITY IN AFRICA

In the modern state of Mali are the remains of Africa's oldest known city – Jenne-Jeno. Situated on the River Niger, it was occupied by iron-working people from about 200 BC. But not until about AD 400 did a settlement develop there. Because of trade across the Sahara Desert (see page 25) Jenne-Jeno became a very important city. The fertile countryside nearby produced food which could be transported by river to other cities, such as Timbuktu on the edge of the Sahara. Gold and other goods were traded farther north. By about the end of the 9th century the city had nearly 1,000 houses – some built in the traditional round style, others square or rectangular, showing the influence of the styles of the Mediterranean and the Near East.

Jenne-Jeno in the year 1000

Temple-pyramid at Chichen Itza

ⓐ TOLTECS AND CHICHEN ITZA

In about 1000 the Toltecs developed the city of Chichen Itza in the Yucatan peninsula of Mexico. According to legend the city was founded by the Toltecs' god-king, Quetzalcoatl, and the biggest building in the city – a temple-pyramid – is dedicated to him. In the Toltecs' capital, Tula, worship of Quetzalcoatl was forbidden. Temple-pyramids were common in Mesoamerica, as were the arenas where a ritual ball game called *tlachti* was played. We know something about the rules for this game from the records of the Spanish invaders in the 16th century. It was like basketball but with important differences. Two teams competed to throw a solid rubber ball through rings on each side of the ball-court. Players were not allowed to use their hands and feet to propel the ball – only their knees, shoulders and arms – and the losing players were beheaded.

950–1000

950 Toltec civilization in Valley of Mexico.
957 Christianity spreads into Russia.
960 Sung Dynasty unites central and southern China.
962 Pope John XII crowns Otto I of Germany the Holy Roman Emperor.
966 State of Poland founded.
967 Fujiwara family take control in Japan.
976 Reign of Byzantine Emperor Basil II begins.
978 Vladimir I founds Russian state at Kiev.
984 Viking settlements founded in Greenland.
985 Rajaraja I begins reign of Chola kingdom in southern India.
998 Hungarian state established.
1000 Thule hunting people spread from Alaska to Greenland.
c1000 Chinese use gunpowder in war.
c1000 Toltecs take over Chichen Itza.
c1000 Northern Iroquoian villages spread to Great Lakes of North America.
c1000 Viking settlements in North America.
c1000 Anasazi farmers build large settlements in American South-west.

1000–1100

c1000 New Zealand first settled.
c1000 Huge stone statues put up on Easter Island in the Pacific.
c1000 Islamic influence spreads into East and West Africa.
1016 Danish King Canute rules England, Denmark and Norway.
1018 Bulgaria taken over as a province of the Byzantine Empire.
1044 First Burmese state established at Pagan.
1055 Seljuk Turks capture Baghdad.
1066 Norman invasion and conquest of England.
1067 Kingdom of Ghana destroyed by Muslims.
1072 Normans invade Scotland.
1077 Embassy of merchants from the Chola kingdom reaches China.
1086 Domesday Book commissioned for England.
1091 Normans conquer Sicily.
1096 First Crusade against Muslims in the Holy Land.
1099 Jerusalem captured by Crusaders. Holy Land divided into four kingdoms.
1100 Anasazi settlements now fortified.

Building the Islamic Empire

In the Near East and around the Mediterranean, the Islamic peoples grew more powerful and further expanded their empire by conquest. Since 750 the Islamic Empire had been ruled by the caliphs of the Abbasid Dynasty from the capital, Baghdad. By the 10th century the empire was divided into a number of caliphates – individual states each ruled by a caliph. The Arabs, who were the founders of Islam, no longer controlled the Islamic Empire.

Within the enlarged Islamic Empire the Seljuk Turks were emerging as a major new force. The Turks had been converted to Islam in 956. During the 11th century they settled in the Middle East and became powerful. In 1055 they captured Baghdad, and their leaders, called sultans, ruled on behalf of the Abbasid Dynasty. Whereas in earlier Muslim states the Turks had merely provided bodyguards and soldiers for Arab rulers, now the power of the new Muslim state rested with Turkish armies supported by Arab and Persian administrators.

Christians against Muslims

The Eastern Christians of Byzantium had lost large parts of their empire to the Muslims. During the reign of the warrior-emperor Basil II, the Byzantines fought the 'infidel' (literally 'unfaithful' – that is non-Christian) and regained some of this lost territory. But in 1071 the Seljuk Turks decisively defeated the Byzantine army at Manzikert now in Armenia. The heart of the Byzantine Empire was now under threat of annihilation by the Muslims as they pushed west towards Constantinople. At the same time the Byzantines lost their last territory in Italy to the invading Norman armies, who also attacked and conquered Britain (see page 33).

WESTERN EUROPE

955 Otto I of Germany defeats the Magyars at the Battle of Lechfeld.
962 Otto I crowned by Pope John XII.
966 State of Poland founded, Mieszko I first king.
982 German victory over Muslims in southern Italy.
987 Hugh Capet elected King of France. Capetian Dynasty founded.
998–1038 Hungarian state established, with Stephen I as first king.
1015 The Dane Canute invades England.
1016–35 Canute is King of England.
1042–66 Edward the Confessor King of England.
1066 Invasion of Normans led by William defeats English at Hastings.
1072 William invades Scotland.
1086 Domesday Book commissioned for England.
1091 Sicily conquered by the Normans.
1096 First Crusade begins.

MIDDLE EAST

957 Christianity spreads in Russia.
961 Byzantine Empire recaptures Crete from Muslims.
963–9 Nicephorus Phocas, Byzantine Emperor, campaigns against the Muslims.
976–1025 Basil II, Byzantine Emperor, defeats the Muslims, Russians, Bulgarians and Normans.
978–1015 Vladimir I sole ruler of the state of Kiev in Russia. He marries a Byzantine princess. Christianity now Kiev's official religion.
1018 Bulgaria becomes a full Byzantine province.
1054 Kievan Russia in decline, invasions of nomads from Asia.
1055 Seljuk Turks capture Baghdad.
1071 Turks defeat Byzantines at Manzikert.
1096 First western Christian Crusade against Muslims in the Holy Land.
1099 Crusaders capture Jerusalem from Muslims.

AFRICA, INDIA

969 Fatimid (Islamic) Dynasty continues revolt against Abbasid rule and conquers Egypt.
985–1014 Rajaraja I rules the Chola kingdom in southern India.
997–1030 Sultan of Ghazni in Turkestan conquers eastern Afghanistan and northern India and rules an Islamic empire.
999 Bagauda is first King of Kano in Nigeria.
c1000 Islamic influence spreads into West Africa and into Nubia.
c1000 West African trading towns (such as Jenne-Jeno) flourish.
1052 Almoravid Dynasty in northern Islamic Africa attacks Ghana.
1054 Muslim conquest of West Africa led by Abdullah ben Yassim.
1056 Almoravids rule in North Africa and Spain.
1067 Kingdom of Ghana destroyed by Almoravids.
1077 Embassy of merchants from the kingdom of Chola in India go to China.

THE FAR EAST

947 Khitans invade northern China and set up the Liao Dynasty.
960 Sung Dynasty unites central and southern China. Capital city at Kaifeng. Prosperous period, trade contacts important by sea throughout South-East Asia and the Indian Ocean. Technology developed – cast iron pagodas produced.
990 Yangtu (Beijing) becomes capital of northern China.
c1000 New Zealand first settled by ancestors of present-day Maoris.
c1000 Enormous head-statues carved and erected on Easter Island on platforms (*ahu*). On Hawaii terraces, courts and platforms (*marae*) built for religious worship.
c1000 Chinese use gunpowder in war.
1044 First Burmese state formed at Pagan.
1075–77 Chinese invasion of Vietnam fails.
1086–88 Civil war in Japan.

◁ The Bayeux Tapestry was probably sewn in England and then taken to Bayeux in France.

▲ NORMAN EXPANSION

The Normans, who were originally the Norsemen or Northmen from Denmark, were warriors who left their place of settlement in Normandy, northern France, to invade Italy and Sicily. They even made attacks on the Byzantine Empire. They are probably best-known for the invasion of England in 1066. A Norman army about 7,000 strong, led by King William of Normandy, defeated the Saxons under King Harold at the Battle of Hastings. The invasion and the battle, in which the English king was wounded and killed, was recorded at the time in the Bayeux Tapestry, part of which is shown here. It gives us an idea of what the Normans' boats, armor and weapons looked like.

THE AMERICAS

950 Two nomadic peoples join together in Mesoamerica to form the Toltecs, based in the Valley of Mexico. Capital city of Tula built.
c1000 Mayan city of Chichen Itza (formerly called Uucilabnal) taken over by Toltecs.
984 Viking Eric the Red reaches Greenland from Iceland.
c1000 Viking settlements in Labrador and Newfoundland.
c1000 Tiahuanaco and Huari empires in the Andes region of South America in decline.
1000 Thule hunting people of the Arctic spread from Alaska to Greenland.
c1000 Northern Iroquoian villages spread to the eastern Great Lakes.
c1000 Anasazi farmers build large settlements in the American South-west.
1100 Anasazi villages now built in protected places – cliffs of the Mesa Verde, or fortified, like Pueblo Bonito.

▶ DOMESDAY BOOK

In 1086 King William of Normandy carried out a survey of all the English lands he had conquered. He wanted to be sure that his subjects were all paying their rents and taxes. This survey came to be known as the Domesday Book. An efficient system of administration already in place in Anglo-Saxon England allowed King William's commissioners to collect information about who owned land at that time. Other information included the number of plow teams in each village as well as lists of livestock, fish-ponds, beehives and salt-works.

Gathering information for the Domesday Book

MONASTERIES

In the Roman Empire in the 3rd century some Christians wanted to devote themselves to God by living and worshipping alone. They became monks (from the Greek word for 'alone', *monos*), who first began to gather together in small communities, called monasteries, in the Egyptian desert. Women who chose a similar way of life became nuns. Monks and nuns gave up the right to marry as well as all the comforts and luxuries of the world outside. Monasteries and nunneries also grew up in the far-off provinces of the Roman Empire, such as Britain. They became places of learning – monks were often the only people who could read and write in a community. Many monasteries followed a religious order – a rule of life – named after a saint. In 909 the Cluniac Order was established at Cluny Abbey (see below) in Burgundy in France. Monasteries soon grew rich and powerful from the lands they were given by kings and the nobility.

△ Little remains of Cluny Abbey today apart from its eight-sided belfry.

◁ The monastery at Cluny in about 1157. Already by 1109 there were 3,000 monks living here.

MONASTERIES

c300 First monasteries and nunneries established in the Egyptian desert.
c340 First monasteries in Italy.
c410 Monastery founded in Marseilles (southern France).
c455 First monks sent to Ireland.
543 St Benedict, founder of the monastery at Monte Cassino, Italy, dies.
597 Augustine sent by the Pope to convert the English.
601 Monastery founded in Canterbury, southern England.
793 Monastery at Lindisfarne, northern England, destroyed by the Vikings.
909 Cluny monastery founded.
927 First monastic church completed at Cluny.
963 Foundation of Aghia Lavra monastery on Mount Athos in northern Greece.
1054 Split between Orthodox (Eastern) and Catholic Church based in Rome.
1070 Monastery founded at Battle, southern England, on site of battle in 1066 between the Normans and English.
1084 Carthusian order founded in Rheims.
1098 Cistercian order founded at Citeaux, Burgundy.
1128 First Cistercian monks settle in England.

Mesa Verde

▲ ANASAZI CLIFF DWELLERS

During the 12th century the Anasazi people of North America began to build their houses in the overhanging cliffs of the mesas (high, long ridges). The most impressive of these settlements is shown here at Mesa Verde, Colorado. Some of the buildings are four stories high with hundreds of rooms. Some served as religious meeting places.

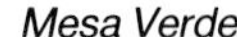

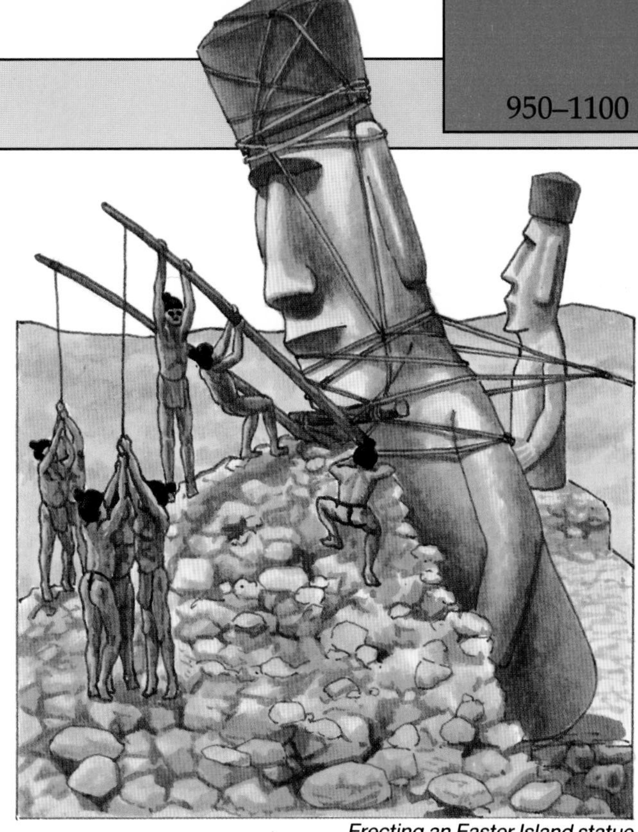

Erecting an Easter Island statue

▲ EASTER ISLAND

Easter Island is in the Pacific Ocean, off the coast of Chile. People had lived on the island since the 4th century, but from about 1000 they began to build rows of enormous stone statues on platforms – long heads with long ears. Six hundred statues have been found there. By about 1600 the stone quarrying and carving had ceased.

In 1095 the Byzantine Emperor Alexius I sent an embassy to Pope Urban II in Rome to ask for help in saving the Christian east from the warriors of Islam. The Pope was already planning to visit France, and from there he appealed to western Christian nations to take part in a 'Holy War' against the Muslims. As a result of his appeal the First Crusade – a military expedition to recover the 'Holy Land' – set off in 1096. By 1099 the holy city of Jerusalem had been recaptured for Christianity. But the fight against the Islamic Empire was a long, drawn-out affair. The full story is told in the next chapter.

The Pacific

Far away in the Pacific, most of the island groups had been settled by about 650. The exception was New Zealand, which had to wait another three centuries. In about 1000, Polynesian farmers, who were the ancestors of the present-day Maoris, came to the islands of New Zealand. The Polynesians reached many islands across the Pacific between New Zealand, Hawaii and Easter Islands. By the time the Europeans reached Polynesia, in the 17th century, there were 35 languages spoken in the region, all related to one introduced in prehistoric times.

Throughout the region, the peoples of the Pacific left behind them numbers of great stone monuments. Some were quite extraordinary – for example, the Easter Island statues (as shown above). Everywhere, stone temples, platforms, upright stones and burial mounds were quite a common sight.

ARAB SCIENCE

The numbers with which we are familiar today were brought to us from the Muslim world. In addition, Arab scientists developed many ideas about medicine, algebra and mathematics, astronomy and navigation. The ideas and inventions of the Greeks and the Romans, which had been passed on to the Eastern Roman Empire in Constantinople, were collected by Muslims as they traded or conquered. Travellers to Muslim lands, such as Spain, brought this knowledge back to Christian Europe.

In the picture below, Muslim seafarers of the 10th century are using an astrolabe to chart their progress. This complex instrument had been invented by the Babylonians more than 1,500 years earlier. Muslim scholars knew about it from a Greek book in the library at Alexandria in Egypt.

▽ An astrolabe measured the positions of the Sun or stars. From this, a ship could tell its own position.

ARAB SCIENCES

630 Muslims take control of Mecca. Most of Arabia converted to the religion of Islam.
636 Muslim army defeats Byzantine forces and takes control of Syria.
c650 Public baths in Muslim towns.
698 Muslims capture Carthage in North Africa.
711 Muslims occupy Spain.
750 All trade by sea between the Red Sea and China controlled by the Muslims.
from 750 Under the Abbasid Dynasty (capital at Baghdad), scholars develop the sciences of mathematics, astronomy and medicine.
751 Paper introduced from China to Muslim Empire.
c800 Windmills in use in Muslim world.
c850 Round towers invented for Muslim castles.
916 Muslim scholar al-Masudi travels from the Gulf along East African coast to Mozambique. Muslim traders settle in East Africa.
c1050 Muslim armies first use hand grenades.
c1250 Muslim doctors first discover how the human heart works (before western doctors).
1150 Papermaking spreads into Europe from Muslim Empire.
1202 Arabic numerals introduced into Europe.

◁ Muslims traders sailed to northern Europe, the Black Sea, and even India and the Far East.

Muslim engineering

On land, Muslims were good planners and designers who knew how to lay out their towns and cities. They were also fine engineers and experts at providing their citizens with a proper water supply – especially public baths and fountains. An 11th-century writer called al-Bakri records that the caliph ordered a survey of the Roman aqueducts in northern Tunisia. From this information the caliph's engineers were able to develop their own, more complex system to meet the people's needs.

△ In the 9th and 10th centuries, Arab astronomers made careful studies and illustrations of the constellations, the groupings of bright stars in the sky, such as Leo above. By the end of the 9th century, al-Khwarizmi, who developed modern algebra and the decimal system, set up a major school of astronomy in Baghdad. About 50 years later, a school of mathematics and astronomy was set up in Toledo, Spain, at the other end of the Muslim world.

◁ A Muslim astrolabe made by al-Kharim Misri in 1236 in Egypt.

NATIONS IN CONFLICT

The period from the 12th to the mid-13th century was one of major change and upheaval. In Europe, the number of people swelled, creating food shortages, while Asia was ravaged by Mongol horsemen. In the Holy Land western Christians led an onslaught against Muslims. Meanwhile, on the American continent, the Incas, who later became immensely powerful (see page 50), founded their legendary city of Cuzco in the Andes in about 1200.

The people of Europe

In 1000 there were about 43 million people living in Europe. Two hundred years later this figure had risen to 73 million. As more towns were built to accommodate more people, the pressure on the countryside to produce more food increased. When the harvest failed or farm animals died in large numbers, people went hungry.

Traveling in Europe and the Mediterranean was neither easy nor safe. Some people, such as merchants, traveled long distances because they had to. They often journeyed to one of the great trading fairs which were becoming popular. Other people sometimes made journeys for their religion. Such journeys were called pilgrimages (see Compostela, page 41).

1110–1190

1100 Thule hunters in the Arctic rapidly spread east and dominate area from Siberia to Greenland.
1106 Henry I of England defeats his brother and becomes Duke of Normandy.
1119 University of Bologna founded.
1119 Order of Knight Templars founded.
1150 University of Paris founded.
1157–82 Waldemar I makes Denmark a major power, subduing the provinces and building castles.
1164 Bishops demand the right to elect kings in Norway.
1168 Toltec city of Tula, Mesoamerica, destroyed by Chichimeca invaders.
1170 University of Oxford founded.
1170 Thomas a Becket, Archbishop of Canterbury, murdered on orders of King Henry II.
1180 Assembly of bishops and dukes in Poland tries to unite the country.
1187 Saladin, leader of the Muslims, recaptures Jerusalem.
1189–99 Richard I, King of England, 'Lionheart'. Campaigns in Europe and goes on the Crusade.
1190 Crusading Order of the Teutonic Knights founded.

1190–1250

1191 Cyprus and some Holy Land towns reconquered by Richard I.
c1200 Power of Chichen Itza declines. New capital built at Mayapan. Decline of Mayan civilization in the Yucatan peninsula.
c1200s Building of 'Gothic' style cathedrals.
c1200 Rock-cut churches built in Ethiopia.
1200 City-states of Hausa in Nigeria founded.
c1200 Aztecs establish small states in Mexico.
1202 Arabic numerals introduced into Europe.
1204 Crusaders capture Constantinople and establish a Latin Empire.
1206 Mongol nomads united by Temujin, who becomes their 'Universal Leader' – the Genghis Khan.
1215 Beijing captured by the Mongols.
1215 English barons force King John to sign the *Magna Carta*.
1221 Mongols invade India.
1227 Genghis Khan dies. His son Ogadei becomes the Great Khan but the Mongol Empire is divided between the four sons of Genghis Khan.
1234 Ogadei overcomes last of the Ch'in Empire in China.
1237–41 Mongol invasions of Poland, Hungary and Russia.

THE MEDIEVAL VILLAGE

In medieval Europe, the way a village was organized depended on where it was situated. In the Mediterranean region, villages were often built on high land, and the houses were of stone. Shown here is a typical village from northern Europe. At one end is the house of the lord of the manor. Central to village life was the church with its own house for the priest. The villagers grew vegetables and kept animals on plots attached to their houses, but they also worked larger fields surrounding the village. These fields were often divided into strips, especially in parts of England, and allocated to the people of the village.

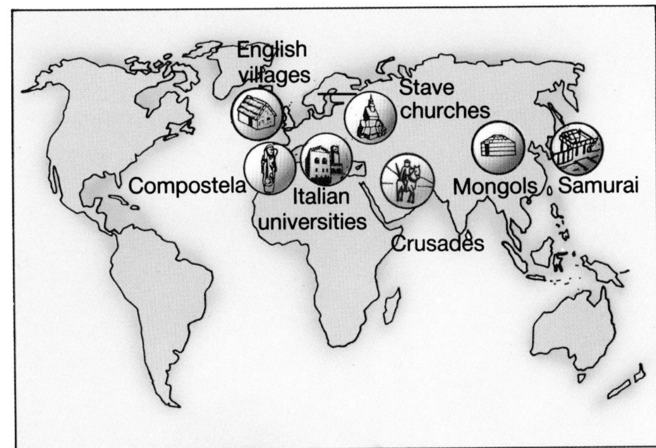

△ In the 12th and 13th centuries many people were on the move. Christians went from Europe to fight Muslims in the Holy Land, and Mongol tribes swept eastward and westward from central Asia.

▷ The church and stream in the medieval village of Wharram Percy in northern England as it is today. In medieval times, around and between the church and stream were the lord of the manor's house and plots of farmers' houses and their gardens set out and built as shown below.

Chaucer's *Canterbury Tales*

The English poet Geoffrey Chaucer (c.1340 to 1400) wrote *The Canterbury Tales*, about the five-day journey of a group of pilgrims travelling from London to Canterbury. This had been a popular place of pilgrimage (see page 12) for English Christians, especially in springtime. Translated into modern English, Chaucer's poem begins 'When in April the sweet showers fall and pierce the drought of March to the root...then people long to go on pilgrimages.

△ A medieval manuscript for law students from Venice, Italy. Teachers at Paris and the older students at Bologna formed themselves into societies to protect their interests. These societies (in Latin *universitates*) became centers of learning.

SCHOOLS AND UNIVERSITIES

The clergy of the Christian Church in medieval Europe were educated and became the teachers of others. Many people, both rich and poor, could not read or write. Schools for children were established as part of monasteries or were set up by bishops. In 1070, a school for the local children of Canterbury in England was founded by the Archbishop of Canterbury. Parish priests in villages and towns also did some teaching. Universities, for more advanced studies, were first founded in the 12th century in France (in Paris) and in Italy (in Salerno, Bologna and Padua).

Christian pilgrims

Pilgrims could often be identified from what they wore. The sculpture of St James on page 41 shows the pilgrim's simple tunic, cloak and wide-brimmed hat (round his neck). The hat offered not only protection from the blazing eastern sun and cold English rain but also an ideal place for pilgrim souvenir badges, which were sold at places like Canterbury and Compostela. Pilgrims carried a staff and a bag in which provisions were kept, as well as a letter of safe conduct from their church. The scallop shell on St James' bag was a sign that he had been to Santiago de Compostela. Other shells, like cockle shells, were used as symbols for other famous shrines. Shells are often found in excavated graves from this period.

A Samurai warrior

ⓐ THE SAMURAI OF JAPAN

There was a special class of warriors, Samurai, in Japan from about the 9th century. The Samurai were fierce, but skilful soldiers who were devoted to duty. In 1185 the military family of the Minamoto took control of Japan and established a feudal government in Kamakuru. By 1192 the Emperor had abdicated and the head of the Minamoto family, Yoritomo, became the country's *shogun* (leader). The aristocratic Samurai warriors lived in defended manor houses, often surrounded by a moat, and controlled the farmland worked by the local population.

WESTERN EUROPE

1106 Henry I of England defeats his brother and becomes Duke of Normandy.
1119 University of Bologna founded.
1130 Norman state established in Sicily.
1150 University of Paris founded.
1154 Henry II becomes King of England and large parts of France.
1170 University of Oxford founded.
1170 Thomas a Becket, Archbishop of Canterbury murdered on the orders of King Henry II.
1189–99 Richard I, King of England. He spends only 7 months in England in 10-year reign.
1197 Richard I, the Lionheart, completes the Chateau Gaillard.
c1200s Building of 'Gothic' style cathedrals.
1202 Arabic numerals introduced into Europe.
1212 Crusade against the Muslims in Spain.
1215 English barons force King John to sign the *Magna Carta*, allowing them to set up a Council.

N. AND E. EUROPE

1140 Vladislav II becomes the king of Bohemia. He establishes strong links with Germany.
1157–82 Waldemar I ('The Great') makes Denmark a major power, subduing the provinces and building castles.
1164 Bishops demand the right to elect the kings of Norway.
1173 King Bela III of Hungary annexes Croatia, Dalmatia and Bosnia.
1180 Assembly of Polish bishops and dukes tries to unite country.
1190 Crusading Order of the Teutonic Knights founded.
1202 Waldemar II takes the throne of Denmark. He adds Norway and coastal lands, such as Estonia, to Danish control.
1226–83 Order of Teutonic Knights sent by the Holy Roman Emperor of Germany, Frederick II, to convert Prussia.
1237–41 Mongols invade Russia, Poland and Hungary.
1241 Swedes now rule Finland.

Religion and conquest

Earlier, the followers of the religion of Islam had conquered large areas of the Near East and even parts of Europe (see pages 22–3). But after 1099, when Jerusalem was recaptured by the Christians, Christian states were set up to safeguard the 'Holy Land'. However, the Christians were by no means always victorious in these religious wars, which went on until well into the 15th century. (see Timechart, page 44).

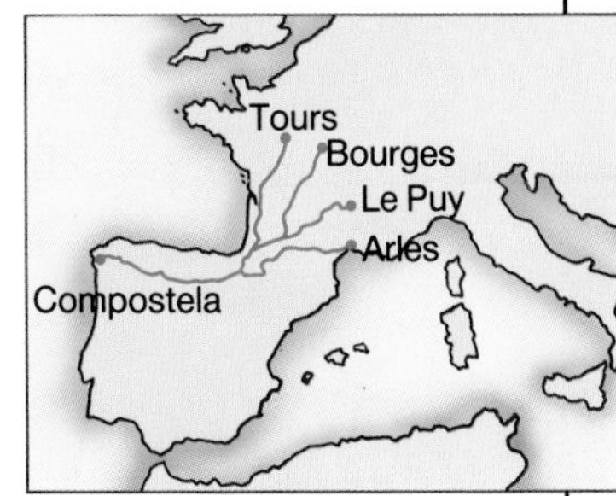

MIDDLE EAST

1119 Order of Knights Templar founded.
1150 Byzantines attempt to recapture Italy.
1169 Muslim Saladin, general of Nur al-Din, administers Egypt.
1171 Saladin overthrows the Fatimid caliphate based in Egypt and founds his Ayyubid Dynasty.
1187 Saladin, with 30,000 soldiers, crosses the River Jordan and recaptures Jerusalem.
1191 Cyprus and some coastal towns of the Holy Land reconquered by Richard the Lionheart.
c1200 Rock-cut churches in Ethiopia.
1200 Rise of the Kingdom of Mali (West Africa).
1200 City-states of Hausa in Nigeria founded.
1204 Crusaders capture Constantinople and establish a Latin Empire.
1244 Jerusalem falls to the Muslims.
1250 Mamluks, special guards employed as Muslim soldiers from southern Russia, control Egypt and Syria.

ASIA, FAR EAST

1162 Temujin (later called Genghis Khan) is born.
1206 Muslim sultanate of Delhi in India founded.
1206 Mongol tribes united by Temujin, who becomes Genghis Khan, the 'Universal Leader'.
1211 Mongols invade the Ch'in Empire of China.
1215 Beijing captured by the Mongols.
1221 Mongols invade India.
1227 Genghis Khan dies. His son Ogadei becomes the Great Khan. The Mongol Empire is divided between the four sons of Genghis.
1234 Ogadei overcomes last of the Ch'in Empire.
1236 Mongols destroy the Kama Bulgars.
1237–41 Mongol invasions of Poland, Hungary and Russia.
1241 Hungarians led by Bela IV defeated by the Mongols. Withdrawal of Mongols on the death of Great Khan Ogadei saves Europe from invasion.
1242 The Mongol Golden Horde established in southern Russia.

THE AMERICAS

1100 Anasazi peoples living in well-defended settlements in American South-west.
1100 Thule hunters in the Arctic rapidly spread east and dominate area from Siberia to Greenland. Their descendants are the modern Inuits (Eskimos).
1150 Anasazi now the most powerful group in the South-west.
1168 Toltec city of Tula destroyed by Chichimeca invaders.
c1200 Power of Chichen Itza declines. New capital built at Mayapan. Decline of Mayan civilization in the Yucatan Peninsula of Mesoamerica.
1200 Legend records the first Inca ruler, Manco Capac, founding the city of Cuzco in the Andes region of South America.
c1200 Large towns inhabited by Chimu people on the coast of northern Peru.
c1200 Aztecs begin to establish small states in Mexico.

Sculpture of St James

▶ MONGOL EMPIRE

Despite their reputation as barbarians, the Mongols were capable of more than looting and destruction. They were a nomadic people, who moved across country driving their cattle, sheep, goats and horses. They ate the meat of their animals and made cheese from the milk, but imported rice and grain. They also produced an alcoholic drink, called *kumiss*, from the milk of mares. They lived in tents, called yerts, made of felt stretched over light wooden frames.

Mongol tribesmen and their yerts

▲ COMPOSTELA

One of the most popular places for Christian pilgrimage in western Europe was Compostela in northern Spain. In about 830 a tomb was discovered there believed to be that of St James (shown above dressed as a pilgrim). Pilgrims from northern Europe took the routes shown through France and Spain. Towns and villages along this route became very rich. By the end of the 11th century Compostela was as important as Rome for a Christian pilgrim.

As well as fighting the Muslims, the Christians who had traveled from western Europe fought against those Christians who were ruled from Constantinople. The capital city of the Byzantine Empire was even sacked by Crusaders in 1204. This clash had little to do with religious differences, more with power and conquest for their own sake.

Meanwhile, Islam continued to expand in other parts of the world. There was a busy trade with Africa, both east and west. The slave trade developed and brought wealth to cities such as Ife. Under the Muslim leader Muhammad Ghuri and his successors, India was invaded by Muslim armies. Sind was conquered and occupied in 1182, followed by Lahore in 1185 and Delhi in 1192. In northern India, and possibly elsewhere, the cultures of the Hindu and Buddhist religions were being destroyed.

Mongols – the threat from the nomads

One of the most remarkable events in world history was the attempt by the Mongols – a nomadic people from the Central Asian steppes – to conquer the world as they knew it. The first great Mongol chief – Genghis Khan – is among the great historical figures whose name is well known to us today.

In 1206 a powerful leader called Temujin united the tribes from the area now known as Mongolia. Temujin later took on the name Genghis Khan, meaning 'Universal Leader'. He led an army of 150,000 fierce warriors who fought on horseback with bows and arrows, spears, swords and battle axes. Using Chinese advisers, they later added siege machines, such as assault towers and giant catapults, to their armory. They slaughtered many thousands, pursued their enemies ruthlessly and rarely left any survivors from a battle. They sacked towns and villages and carried off one-tenth of the property and population remaining in them.

Scandinavian stave church

Ⓐ STAVE CHURCHES

Today only a few of the Christian churches built between 1000 and 1300 in Scandinavia are still standing. Of the 700 thought to have existed in Norway, only 25 are left. The illustration above is of Borgund Church, at Søgne, in western Norway. It was built in about 1150, and is made entirely of wood, including the roof tiles. Churches like this are called stave meaning 'wooden-planked'. The plan of this church is very simple, with a rectangular nave (for the worshippers) and a square chancel (for the priest and the altar). On the outside there are intricate carvings and decoration. Most of the wooden village churches surviving in Scandinavia are much plainer. There is also an example of a wooden church in the east of England.

By the time of Genghis Khan's death in 1227, the Mongol conquests had created the largest empire the world had ever seen, the Khan and his sons having fought their way east to capture China and west as far as the Caspian Sea. The westward expansion continued for another 30 years or more.

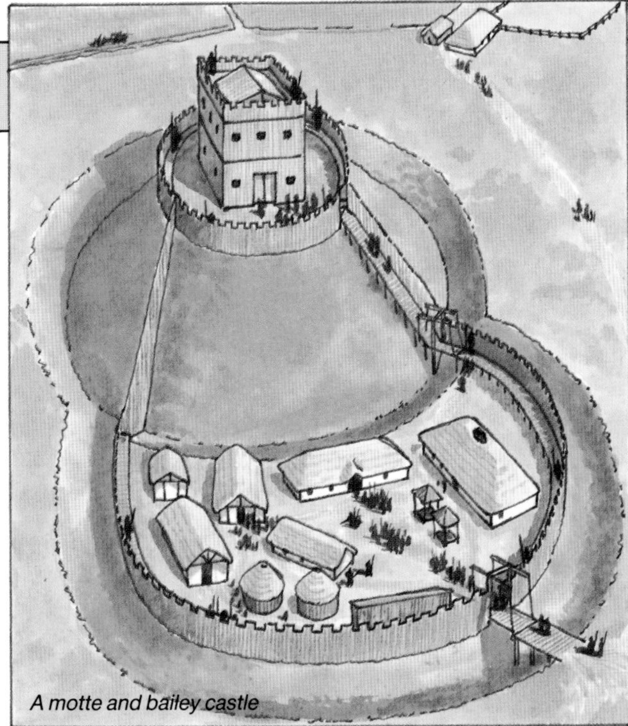

A motte and bailey castle

△ The lord of the manor made the local people build the castle – digging the ditches and piling up the huge mound. The defensive walls, gates and buildings were made of wood.

▷ The central tower, or *donjon*, of Falaise Castle in France dates to the early 11th century. The castle was the birthplace of William the Conqueror. It overlooks the River Orne.

Norman castle in the 12th century

▲▶ CASTLE BUILDING

The first medieval castles in Europe had a large mound of earth (shaped like a cone) with a building (usually of wood) on top (see above). This motte, as it was called, was where the lord or king lived. Below it, and enclosed by a wall or fence, was the bailey, where the retainers and soldiers lived. The motte and bailey type of castle was introduced into England when the Normans invaded. Castles built of stone were obviously stronger against attack. On the right is what the castle at Rochester in southern England may have looked like in the 12th century. The motte has been replaced by a larger building to live in called a keep. To protect the keep and all the buildings in the bailey there are high stone walls with towers at intervals and heavily defended gates.

CASTLES

9th and 10th centuries – Saxon defended settlements known as *burhs*.
10th century Motte and bailey castles first constructed.
c950 Earliest known castle at Doue-la-Fontaine, France.
1066 Norman castles introduced into England.
1196–8 Richard I builds Chateau-Guillard on the borders of Normandy on his return from the Crusades.
1223 Louis VII of France controls 144 castles.
from 1277 Edward I, King of England, builds 14 castles to help conquer Wales.
1320 Cannon introduced into warfare affects castle design. From then on, castle walls built low and thick.

THE CRUSADES

The Turks have overrun the eastern Christians right up to the Mediterranean Sea. They have conquered them, slaughtering and capturing many, destroying churches and laying waste the kingdom of God.

This was part of the preaching of Pope Urban II as he called upon the Christians in France to make a crusade – a 'war of the cross' – against the 'infidel' Muslims.

First Crusade

About 40,000 people went on the First Crusade from Europe, reaching Constantinople in 1096. On 15 July 1099 the army from the west captured Jerusalem.

The Crusaders quickly set up four states in the Holy Land, from Edessa to Jerusalem (see map opposite). The states were ruled by a feudal system (see page 46) similar to the one used in Europe. Many Crusaders stayed on to settle in these Christian states, taking over the towns and building new settlements in the countryside.

Muslims fight back

By the late 12th century the Muslims, led by Saladin, began to push the Crusaders out. The Third Crusade, launched by Richard I of England and Philip II of France, failed to recapture Jerusalem, which had fallen to the Muslims in 1187. More Crusades were called for up until the middle of the 15th century.

Manuscript illustration of the crusader siege of Jerusalem

THE CRUSADES

1095 Pope Urban II travels through France calling for a crusade.
1096 First Crusade leaves and reaches Constantinople.
1098 Antioch besieged and captured.
1099 Jerusalem captured.
1119 Knights Templar ('of the Temple') founded to defend pilgrims on the road to Jerusalem.
c.1130 Hospitallers (Knights of St John) set up.
1144 Edessa recaptured by Muslims.
1145 Second Crusade proclaimed.
1148 Second Crusade army defeated at Damascus.
1163–9 Christians from Jerusalem attack Egypt.
1187 Saladin, Sultan of Egypt, annihilates a Christian army at Hattin and recaptures Jerusalem. Third Crusade proclaimed.
1190 King Richard I ('Lionheart') of England and King Philip II of France set off on Crusade.
1191 Cyprus conquered, coastal towns recaptured.
1197–8 German Crusade recaptures more coastal lands.
1202 Fourth Crusade sails from Venice.
1204 Constantinople sacked by Crusaders. Latin (Western) emperor crowned. The following winter southern Greece is conquered.
1212 Children's Crusade: several thousand child Crusaders reach Alexandria and are sold as slaves.
1217 Fifth Crusade to conquer Egypt.
1221 Crusaders forced to leave Egypt.
1248–54;1270 Crusades of Louis IX of France; captured and ransomed on first crusade; crusaders struck down by disease and Louis dies on second crusade.
1291 Last Latin states in Holy Land captured by Mamluk Muslims.
1309 Popular crusades launched in Europe. Knights Hospitallers move headquarters to Rhodes.
1398–1400 Crusades to defend Constantinople.
1425 Mamluk Muslims attack Cyprus.
1453 Ottoman Turks capture Constantinople.

▷ Crusader footsoldiers used spears, crossbows and large siege engines. Crusaders brought to Europe new military ideas from the Muslims and Byzantines.

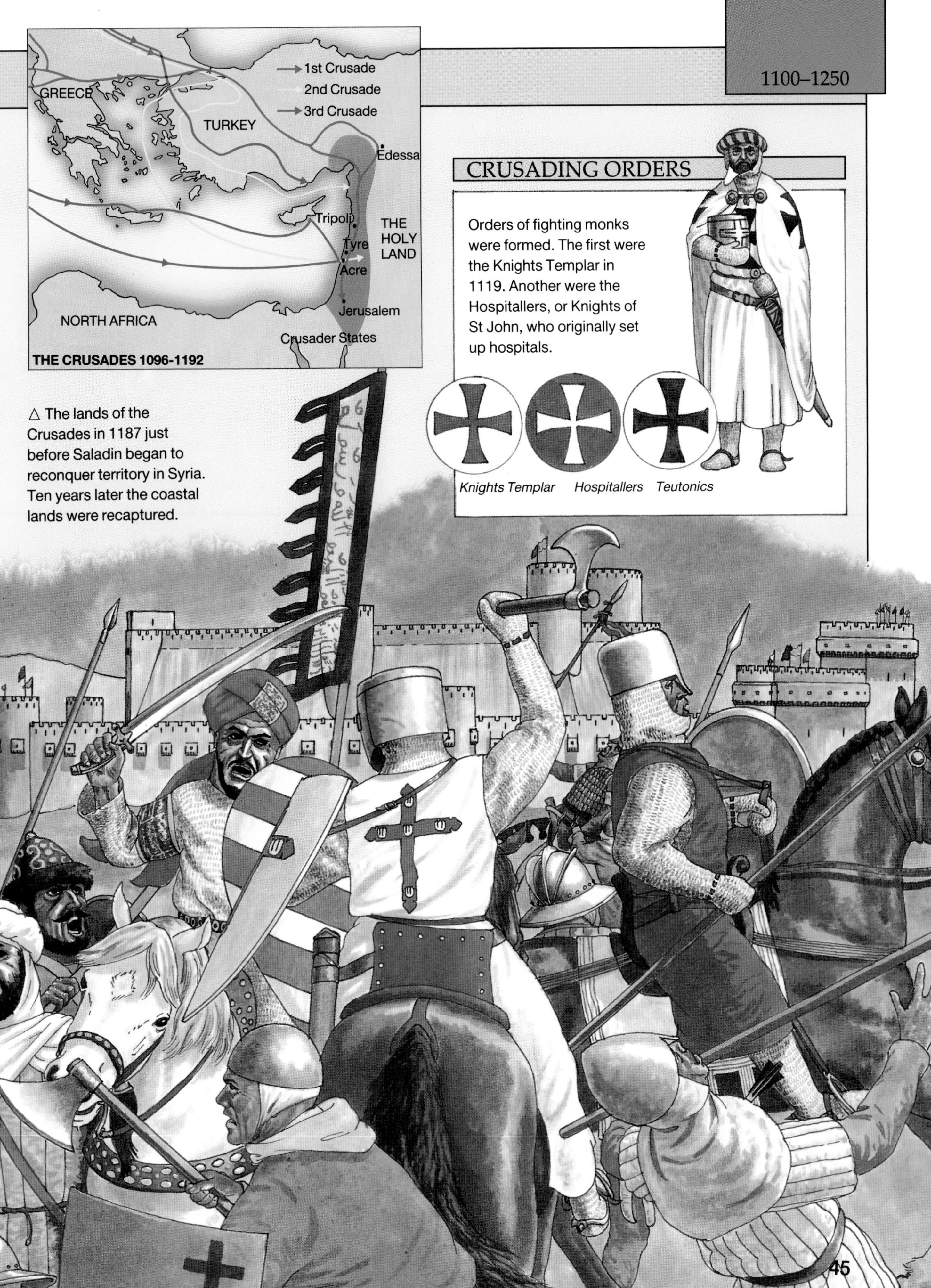

△ The lands of the Crusades in 1187 just before Saladin began to reconquer territory in Syria. Ten years later the coastal lands were recaptured.

CRUSADING ORDERS

Orders of fighting monks were formed. The first were the Knights Templar in 1119. Another were the Hospitallers, or Knights of St John, who originally set up hospitals.

WAR, REBELLION, PLAGUE

Life in Europe altered dramatically for many people during the 13th and 14th centuries. In western Europe in 1337 a war began between France and England which raged for a whole century – it is called The Hundred Years' War.This was also a time of natural disasters such as the Black Death – a terrible plague that swept across Europe killing millions of people. The effects of the plague and growing discontent caused many people in Europe to rise up against their governments. People were also beginning to find out more about other parts of the world.

The countries of Eastern Europe

In eastern Europe many people still lived in small, scattered farming communities. Thus they had little contact with other people, and so the Black Death did not reach them. When Poland, Hungary and Lithuania all expanded and modernized in the 14th century, they encountered the Ottoman Turks on their frontiers. The Ottomans (see page 51) were themselves rapidly expanding and their empire now stretched to the borders of Hungary. Farther east, the warrior king of Samarkand, who was known as Timur (or Tamerlane), destroyed the Golden Horde of the Mongols (see page 42) and scored a series of victories over the Ottomans. These defeats for the Ottomans were so severe that they did not attempt another invasion for 50 years.

The feudal system

Around the year 1000 a political system known as feudalism began in western Europe. In each country, the king gave land to his most powerful nobles in return for their oath of loyalty to serve him and oppose his enemies. The nobles, in turn, gave land to their knights, who shared this land, called a fief, among the ordinary people. They were the peasants, who lived on the land and paid rents but also had to work for their lord, the knight, and fight for him when ordered to do so. Some of the worst-off peasants had neither freedom nor land and received only food, which they grew themselves, in return for their hard work in the fields.

The feudal system was established first in France and Germany, from where it was introduced into England, Sicily and the Holy Land by the Normans. There was also feudalism in parts of Italy and Spain.

▽ Plagues raged through western Europe and unrest among its populations was common. The Islamic people called the Ottomans dominated the eastern Mediterranean and extended their empire.

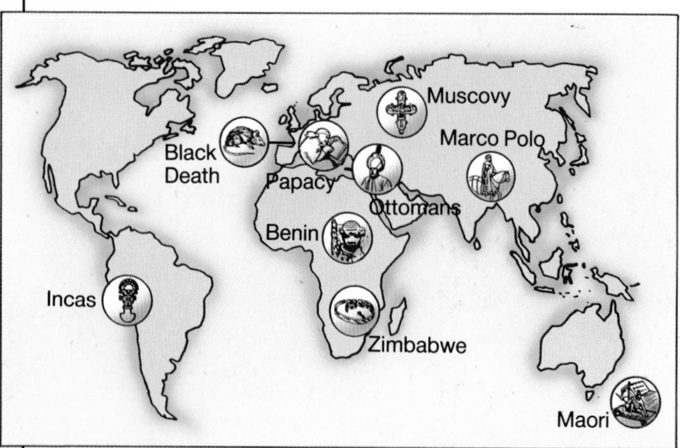

1250–1310

c1250 Berbers establish states in North Africa.
1262 Iceland and Greenland conquered by Norway.
1263 Death of Alexander Nevski in Russia.
1264 Kublai Khan founds the Yuan Dynasty in China.
1270 Louis IX, King of France, dies on Crusade in Tunis.
1275 Marco Polo arrives in China from Venice.
1290 Osman I declares himself Sultan of the Turks and founds the Ottoman Empire.
c1300 Rise of the kingdom of Benin in Nigeria.
1309 Pope moves his residence from Rome to Avignon, France.

1310–1400

1328 Duke Ivan I begins expansion of Moscow.
1337 Start of Hundred Years' War.
c1341 Black Death begins in Asia.
1345 Rise of the Aztecs.
1345 Ottoman Turks cross into Europe.
1346 English defeat the French at the Battle of Crécy.
1347 Start of the Black Death in Europe.
c1350 Firearms first used in Europe.
c1350 Maori people build fortified settlements in New Zealand.
1358 Peasant rebellion in France.
1368 Ming Dynasty founded in China.
1381 Peasants' revolt in England.

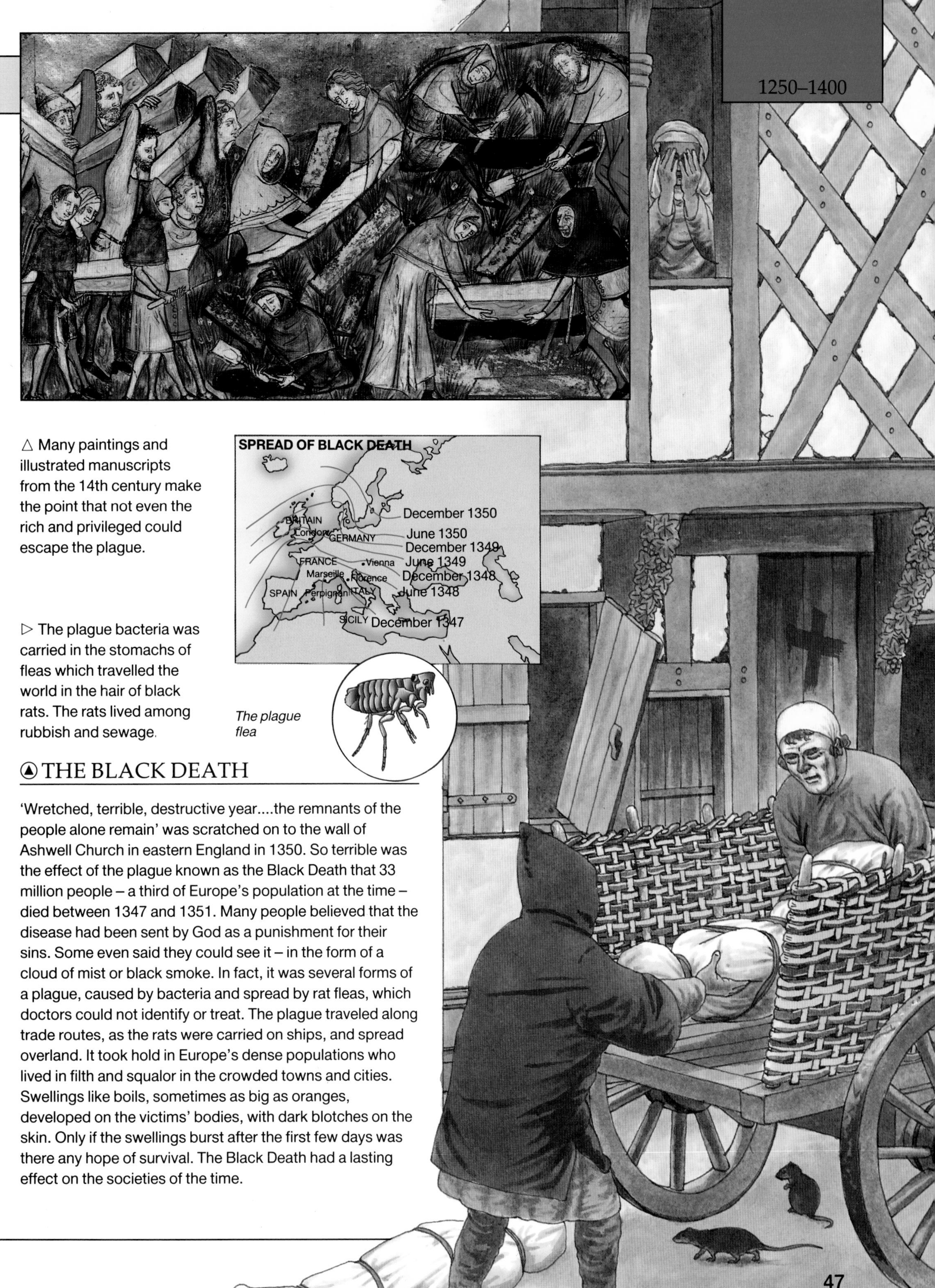

△ Many paintings and illustrated manuscripts from the 14th century make the point that not even the rich and privileged could escape the plague.

▷ The plague bacteria was carried in the stomachs of fleas which travelled the world in the hair of black rats. The rats lived among rubbish and sewage.

▲ THE BLACK DEATH

'Wretched, terrible, destructive year....the remnants of the people alone remain' was scratched on to the wall of Ashwell Church in eastern England in 1350. So terrible was the effect of the plague known as the Black Death that 33 million people – a third of Europe's population at the time – died between 1347 and 1351. Many people believed that the disease had been sent by God as a punishment for their sins. Some even said they could see it – in the form of a cloud of mist or black smoke. In fact, it was several forms of a plague, caused by bacteria and spread by rat fleas, which doctors could not identify or treat. The plague traveled along trade routes, as the rats were carried on ships, and spread overland. It took hold in Europe's dense populations who lived in filth and squalor in the crowded towns and cities. Swellings like boils, sometimes as big as oranges, developed on the victims' bodies, with dark blotches on the skin. Only if the swellings burst after the first few days was there any hope of survival. The Black Death had a lasting effect on the societies of the time.

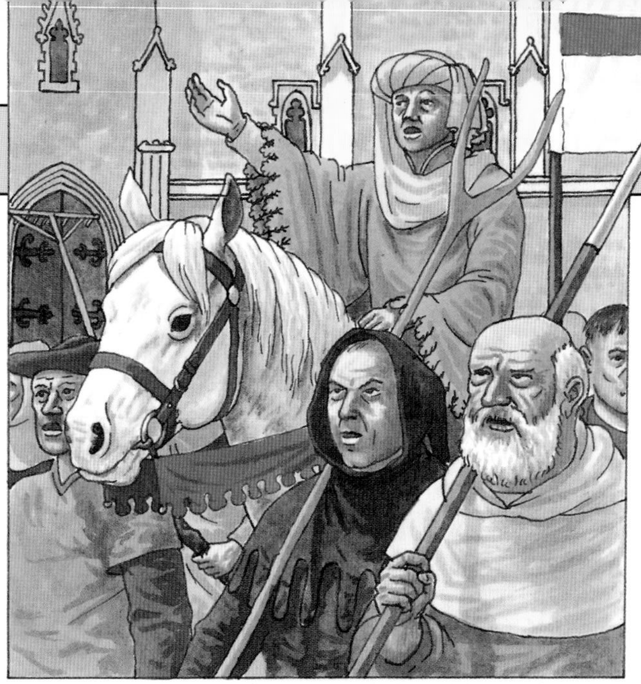
Farmers march through London in protest

Rebellions in western Europe

Gradually, feudalism bred discontent, as people became dissatisfied with a system in which only the king could make the important decisions that affected their lives. In 1215 the powerful barons in England forced their monarch, King John, to sign the Magna Carta ('Great Charter'). This gave the nobles the right to set up a Council for the purpose of advising the King. Similar systems grew up in France, Germany and Spain.

By the late 14th century discontent among the common people had grown into revolution in England, Germany, France, Italy and the Netherlands. The Black Death and other diseases had taken their toll on populations, so that often there were too few people left to work the land. This led to food shortages and to demands by the peasants for more money. Big landowners were forced to break up their estates and sell them off as small farms. New taxes imposed by the landlords sparked off rebellion in many European cities.

PEASANTS' REVOLTS IN ENGLAND

During the 14th century many peasants across Europe began to rebel against their landlords and the authority of kings and the Church. In England trouble flared up in the summer of 1381. For years the peasants had been heavily taxed to pay for wars in France. Two large armies of farmers and farmworkers marched to London to protest. On that occasion King Richard II, who was only 14 years' old at the time, met the rebels and persuaded them to return home. The rebel leader, Wat Tyler, was killed in a skirmish, and there was rioting in many towns throughout England.

WESTERN EUROPE

1250 Collapse of imperial power in Germany and Italy.
1252 Minting of gold florin in Florence.
1262 Iceland and Greenland conquered by Norway.
1290 Spectacles invented in Italy.
1309 Pope moves from Rome to Avignon.
1314 Robert Bruce, King of Scotland, defeats the English at Bannockburn.
1337 Beginning of the Hundred Years' War.
1340 Birth of Chaucer.
1347 Start of Black Death.
c1350 Firearms first used in Europe.
1358 Peasant rebellion in France.
1360 First francs coined in France
1369 Building of the Bastille in Paris.
1377 Pope Gregory XI returns from Avignon to Rome.
1381 Peasants' revolt in England.

N. AND E. EUROPE

1263 Death of Alexander Nevski in Russia.
1273 Rudolf of Hapsburg becomes Holy Roman Emperor.
1278 Bohemia and Moravia under the control of Holy Roman Empire.
1320 Poland reunited.
1328 Duke Ivan I begins expansion of Moscow.
1343 Teutonic Knights occupy Estonia.
1345 Ottoman Turks cross into Europe.
1348 University founded in Prague.
1354 Ottoman Turks capture Gallipoli, their first possession in Europe.
1355 Charles IV of Luxembourg becomes Holy Roman Emperor.
1361 Serbs defeated by the Ottomans.
1386 Poland and Lithuania united.
1389 Ottoman Turks defeat Serbs, Bulgars, Bosnians, Wallachians and Albanians at the Battle of Kossovo.

MIDDLE EAST

c1250 Berbers establish a number of states in North Africa.
1250 Ayyubid Dynasty in Egypt succeeded by Mamluk Dynasty.
1250 Baghdad destroyed by the Mongols.
1260-77 Rule of the Baibar sultans in Egypt.
1260 Mongols take Damascus but are beaten by Egyptians at Ain Jalut.
1268 Baibars take Jaffa, Antioch and Beirut from the Christians.
1281 Beginning of the reign of Turkish chief Osman I.
1290 Osman I declares himself Sultan of the Turks and founds the Ottoman Empire.
c1300 Rise of the kingdom of Benin in Nigeria.
1324 Mansa Musa, King of Mali, in West Africa, visits Cairo.
1397 Portuguese reach the Canary Islands.

ASIA, FAR EAST

1251 Grandson of Genghis Khan, Hulagu, conquers Persia and establishes the Il-Khan Empire.
1264 Kublai Khan founds the Yuan Dynasty in China.
1274 Mongols attempt to invade Japan.
1275 Marco Polo arrives in China from Venice.
1279 Mongols conquer southern China.
1281 The Mongols' fleet is destroyed by a storm.
1293 First Christian missionaries reach China.
1307 First Christian archbishop in Beijing.
1333 Civil war breaks out in Japan.
c1341 Black Death begins in Asia.
1349 Chinese expand into South-East Asia, first settlement in Singapore.
1368 Ming Dynasty founded in China.
1369 Timur (also known as Tamerlane) rules the Mongols.

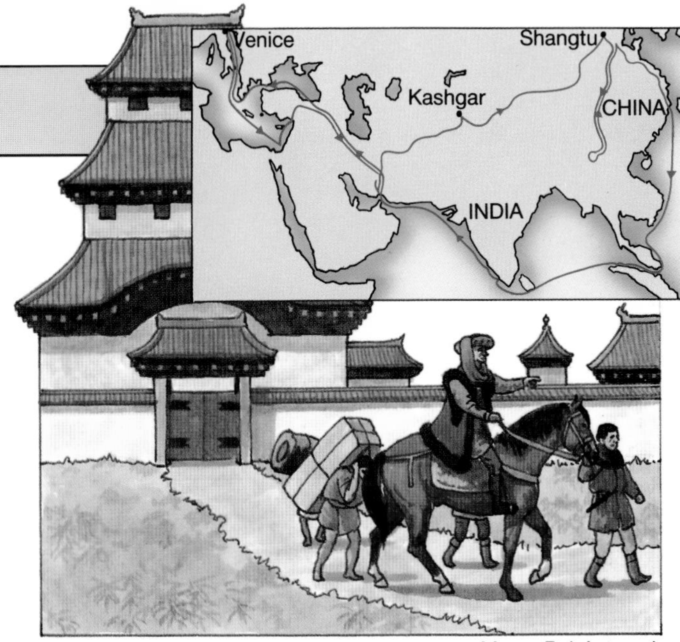

Marco Polo's travels

MARCO POLO IN CHINA

Till the end of the 13th century Europeans knew little about China. Then in 1298, an extraordinary book was published. Called *Description of the World*, it was written by Marco Polo, who, at 21, had traveled to China in 1275 with his father Nicolo and his uncle Maffeo, both of them merchants from Venice who had been to China before. They were liked by the Mongol leader, Kublai Khan, and with his permission traveled freely through China for 20 years. Europeans were astounded to read Marco Polo's account of a country that was wealthier and more advanced than most of Europe.

Benin sculpture

BENIN CIVILIZATION

Lying deep in the rainforests of what is now Nigeria in West Africa are the remains of the city of Benin. There was probably a settlement here by the 12th century, but from the next century onwards the city grew larger. It was surrounded by a massive earth wall nearly 8 miles in length. Benin was ruled by the *Oba* – a king who was also the religious leader. There were huge numbers of other earthworks outside the city, in the nearby villages that were controlled from Benin. Benin's wealth was based on trade, especially of slaves. The kingdom reached its peak in the 16th century.

AMERICAS, PACIFIC

c1200–1300 Early Inca period in Peru.
1276–99 Drought in the American South-west.
c1300 Pueblo cliff settlements in North America abandoned. Arrival of Athabascan Indians from the north-west.
c1300 Natural food supplies drastically decline in North Island, New Zealand. People begin to cultivate more crops.
1345 Rise of the Aztec civilization. Foundation of the city of Tenochtitlan by Chief Tenoch on islands in Lake Texcoco.
c1350 Maori people on North Island, New Zealand build fortified settlements.
c1352 Acamapitzin becomes first king of the Incas.

GREAT ZIMBABWE

The name Zimbabwe comes from the word *dzimba* meaning houses, in the language of the Shona people of East Africa. They built an extraordinary settlement in the 10th or 11th centuries at the site of Great Zimbabwe in the modern country of Zimbabwe. By the 14th century it had grown into a town of about 3,000 people. These were mainly cattle farmers but also included skilled goldsmiths. The people of Great Zimbabwe built huge enclosures (perhaps for religious gatherings) and a tall conical tower.

Great Zimbabwe in about 1350

A Maori hilltop settlement

The Inca capital Cuzco

ⓐ THE INCAS AT CUZCO

The capital city of the Inca Empire was Cuzco in the central Andes. Inca legends told how the first Inca ruler, Manco Capac, founded the city in 1200. As the Incas captured more territory in the Andes, they took the children of local chiefs to Cuzco as hostages. Here they were educated in Inca ways and returned to their own lands. The city of Cuzco was situated between two rivers with a huge central plaza called *Haucaypata*, meaning 'holy place'. Looking down on the city was the great fortress of Sacsahuaman with some 10,000 warriors.

ⓐ MAORI DEFENDED HILLTOPS

From about 1000 the Pacific islands now called New Zealand were occupied by the ancestors of the present- day Maoris. The people were hunters and food-gatherers who also cultivated crops. Agriculture developed especially on the North Island, where, from about 1300, the population grew. People also began to make war on each other and from about 1350 built defended hilltop settlements, called *pa*. Often they chose extinct volcanic craters as suitable sites. They constructed banks and ditches, which they strengthened with wooden walls and platforms.

Beyond Europe

For a long time most people in Europe were unaware of far-off parts of the world even though goods had been traded across continents for centuries. During the Crusades (see page 44) the eastern Mediterranean and North Africa became well known to the western armies who fought there. It was the Mongols who had brought the Far East to the very edge of Europe, and in 1245 a monk was sent from Rome to introduce them to Christianity. Trade was even more important as a communication channel with the Far East. By the end of the 13th century detailed reports about China were reaching western Europe (see Marco Polo in China, page 49).

Africa and trade

Despite trading links with Africa, people in western Europe knew little about the continent beyond the Sahara. Important and rich civilizations had grown up there, especially in West Africa. By 1400 the Kingdom of Mali, which had been created about 200 years earlier, was the major exporter of gold to Europe. The area was also rich in spices, ebony (a very hard wood) and ivory. These along with slaves were sold to Mediterranean traders in exchange for glassware, pottery, beads, silk, saffron and salt.

From the 9th century Arab merchants lived prosperously on the East African coast in thriving Islamic cities. They traded with countries as far south as Great Zimbabwe (see page 49), offering luxury goods from the Islamic world, India and China in return for gold, copper, iron, ivory and slaves. Gold, which was shipped out to Islamic countries from the port of Sofala, east of Great Zimbabwe, was an especially important export.

13th-century Novgorod

▲ ALEXANDER OF NOVGOROD

In the 13th century Russia was threatened by the great Mongol hordes from the east as well as by invasions from the west. When the Swedes attacked Russia in 1240, they were defeated by the young prince Alexander Yarolslavski on the banks of the River Neva. He afterwards took the name Nevski in memory of his victory. Two years later Alexander defeated an army of Teutonic Knights, a German Crusading force. The city of Novgorod, shown above, was the capital of Alexander's state. He negotiated with the Mongols to let the Russian people live in peace.

▼ THE MEDIEVAL POPES

The earliest Christians believed that God was represented on Earth by his Bishop in Rome – the Pope – a belief that is still held by some Christians today. During the 11th and 12th centuries there were struggles between the popes and the emperors of the Holy Roman Empire. For this reason, between 1305 and 1377 the popes resided in Avignon in France rather than in Rome. In 1378 the two opposing sides set up rival popes – one based in Rome and the other in Avignon. This split the western Christian world in two, with Scotland, France, Spain, southern Italy and Sardinia supporting the Avignon pope.

A medieval pope and his clergy

◀ THE OTTOMAN EMPIRE

By the late 13th century the Ottomans, who were Muslims, had taken control of Anatolia (modern Turkey). There was little opposition from the Byzantine Empire, which was weak after the Fourth Crusade (see page 44), or from the Mongols, who had retreated into Iran. The Ottoman Turks waged a holy war against non-Muslims and made them part of their growing empire. In the 14th century they seized Bulgaria and Serbia (shown here) and in 1453 they took Constantinople, ending hundreds of years of Roman rule. From there, they moved down into Greece, and imposed Turkish rule.

A MEDIEVAL TOWN

Some towns in medieval Europe were survivors from the Roman period, while others grew out of villages or were newly built. In the 12th century many new towns were founded, including more than 100 in England and Wales after the Norman Conquest (see page 33). Most towns were small, with populations of up to 20,000. Large, important towns had a cathedral. By 1500, Paris, then the biggest town in Europe, had about 80,000 inhabitants.

Walls and town space

Medieval towns usually had a wall around them and gates for protection. The town authorities were often reluctant to extend the area because building work was expensive and time-consuming. The new walls of Florence in Italy, for example, were begun in 1290 and took 44 years to complete. For these reasons, there was often a shortage of space in the town, with buildings close together and narrow streets and alley-ways.

Markets and industry

Medieval towns had their market-places where goods could be exchanged or sold. There were also many trades and industries in towns. From the 13th century, guilds – associations of tradesmen or craftsmen – were common. Some towns became famous for a particular industry or service, such as Genoa, in Italy, for its banking, or Lavenham, in England, for its wool trade.

▽ A typical medieval town. Towns were divided into a number of parishes, each with its own church. Most other buildings, and houses, were of wood.

MEDIEVAL TOWNS

c1000 Paris becomes the permanent capital of France.
1066 Norman conquest of England. Many new towns founded.
c1075 Black Forest region of Germany settled. Three major towns founded by c1120.
1160 Beginning of Gothic style of architecture.
1194 Chartres cathedral rebuilt in Gothic style.
by 1190 More than 100 new towns founded in England and Wales.
1210 Reims cathedral begun.
c1290 Beginning of the building of a wall around Florence, Italy.

△ ▽ The cathedral in Bourges (above) in central France was built in the mid-13th century in the High Gothic style. Towns used their own seals for documents. The 13th century seal (below) of Gravelines on the northern coast of France shows the town's patron saint.

EXPLORATION AND CHANGE

From the 15th century, Europeans set out to discover new lands, where they traded with the local people but often also conquered them. In Europe itself, England's attempt to conquer France failed after 100 years of fighting. In the Far East, China grew prosperous after expelling the Mongol invaders.

Europe and the Americas

Once the Aztecs had arrived in the Valley of Mexico at the beginning of the 14th century, they quickly established themselves as the most powerful people in the land. By the end of the 15th century they had conquered a huge empire. In South America, from 1483 the Incas, under their emperor Pachacuti, also built an empire, stretching from Colombia to Argentina.

These American civilizations were wiped out by Europeans in the early 16th century. Portugal and Spain, in particular, made voyages across the Atlantic and 'discovered' the Americas. There followed invasions first by merchants, and then by armies, who massacred the people or made slaves out of them and also brought disease. Hernando Cortes began his conquest of the Aztecs in Mexico in 1519, and Francisco Pizarro had conquered the Incas in Peru by 1534.

New dynasty in China

The 15th century also marked a turning point in the history of the Far East. The Mongols were finally driven out of China and a new dynasty was founded (see Beijing in the Ming Dynasty, page 55). Under the Ming Emperors the countryside was revived, the population increased and cities were filled with beautiful buildings. Industry and trade grew, and voyages of exploration began. In 1405 the admiral Cheng Ho sailed as far south as Java and west to India and Africa.

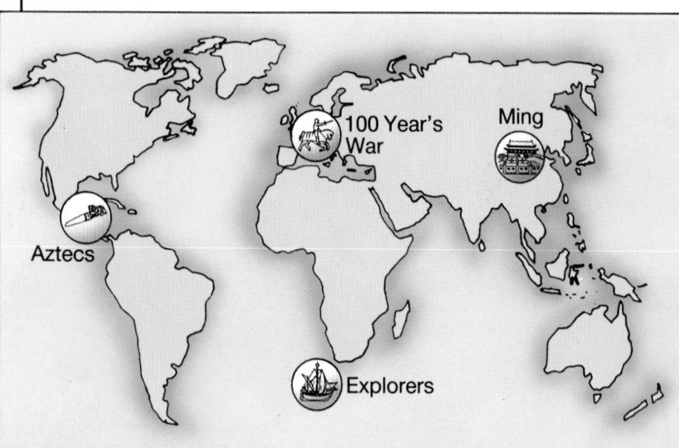

△ Civilizations across the world discovered each other. The Europeans sailed to the Americas, and the Chinese made contact with Asia, Africa and the Middle East. At the same time, there were long and bitter wars – between France and England, and in Japan, while the Chinese invaded Mongolia and Vietnam.

1400–1450

1405–33 Chinese admiral Ch'iu Fu's diplomatic voyages to Java, India, Persia, Arabia and Africa.
1410 Poles defeat the Teutonic Knights at the Battle of Tannenberg.
1415 English defeat the French at the Battle of Agincourt.
1415 Portuguese capture the town of Ceuta, North Africa, and begin voyages around African coasts.
1421 Capital of China moved to Beijing. Great Wall of China extended.
1428 Joan of Arc begins campaigning against English forces in France.
1428 Alliance formed by three cities gives Aztecs control of Valley of Mexico.
1431 Joan of Arc burned at the stake by French clergy who supported the English claim to the throne.
1436 French, under Charles VII, recapture Paris.
1439 Official separation of the Greek and Russian Orthodox churches.
1445 Portuguese reach the mouth of the River Congo, central Africa.
1445 First printed book (a Bible) in Europe produced by the German Johann Gutenberg.

1450–1500

1453 Constantinople falls to the Ottoman Turks. End of the Byzantine Empire.
1453 End of Hundred Years' War between England and France.
1474 William Caxton begins printing books in England.
1477 Wars between the provinces in Japan begin. They last for a century.
1480 Ivan III refuses to pay tribute to the Mongols, drives them out of Moscow and declares himself Tsar of Russia.
1486 Beginning of expansion of Aztec Empire to Pacific Coast and Guatemala.
1487 Portuguese Bartolomeu Diaz sails around the Cape of Good Hope, South Africa.
1492 Granada, last Muslim stronghold in Spain, reconquered by Christian forces.
1492 Christopher Columbus reaches the Bahamas from Europe.
1494 Treaty signed by Spain and Portugal divides up the New World between them.
1497 Portuguese Vasco da Gama sails to India via the Cape of Good Hope.
1499 Amerigo Vespucci begins exploration of South American coast.

100 YEARS' WAR

The Hundred Years' War was the name given to the campaigns and battles between the French and the English from 1337 to 1453. Edward III invaded France in 1339 and soon won a number of battles. Edward's successor, Henry V, won famous victories at Agincourt and Harfleur. For a long time, the French had no answer to the English archers, who could rain arrows down on them from a distance. But eventually the English were driven out.

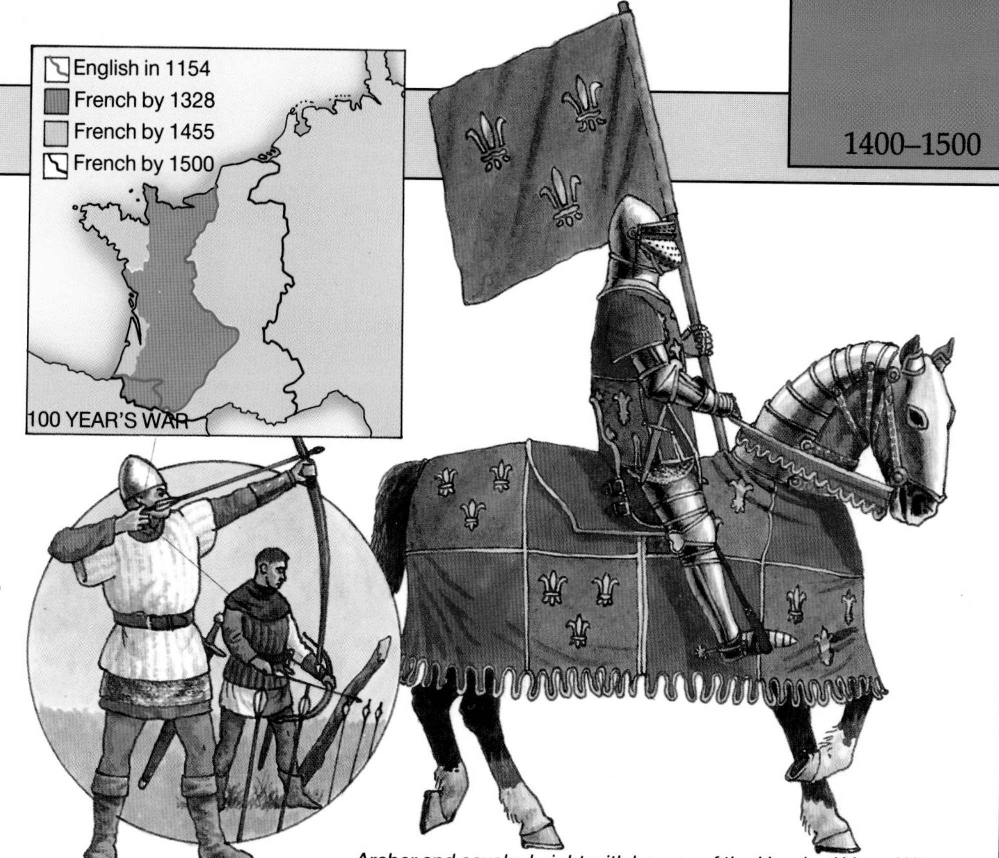

Archer and cavalry knight with banner of the Hundred Years' War

THE AZTECS

The Aztecs themselves told how they came from the north to Lake Texcoco in the Valley of Mexico around 1300. Then, in 1345, they settled on some islands in Lake Texcoco and built their city of Tenochtitlan. They grew so powerful by fighting other peoples that in 1428 they controlled the whole of the Valley of Mexico. By 1500 the Aztecs were in charge of an empire of 10 million people. Not only were they warlike, but they also used to sacrifice some of their captives to their gods. Their capital, Tenochtitlan (see below) had more than 500,000 inhabitants and each day about 60,000 people came there to trade.

The Aztec capital, Tenochtitlan

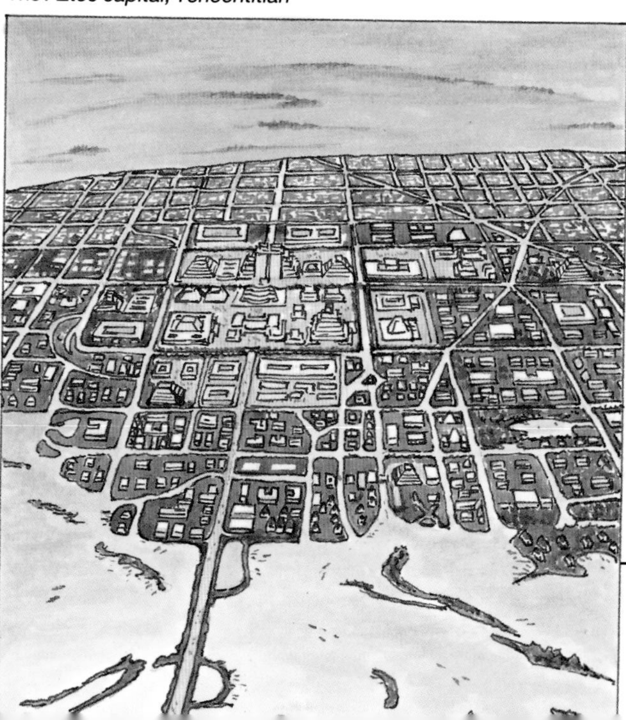

BEIJING IN THE MING DYNASTY

In China, in 1368 a Buddhist monk, Chu Yuan-chang, overthrew the rule of the Mongols and established a new dynasty – the Ming Dynasty – at Nanking. Within 20 years its rulers had driven the Mongols out of China completely. The third emperor of the Ming Dynasty, Young Le, decided to move the capital to Beijing. From 1404 the city was rebuilt as three enclosures protected by walls. The outer city, later called the Chinese City, had many houses and temples. An enormous gate in the northern wall led to the inner city. At its center was the walled-off area reserved for the emperor himself – the Forbidden City.

The Forbidden City, Beijing

Portuguese explorers in Africa

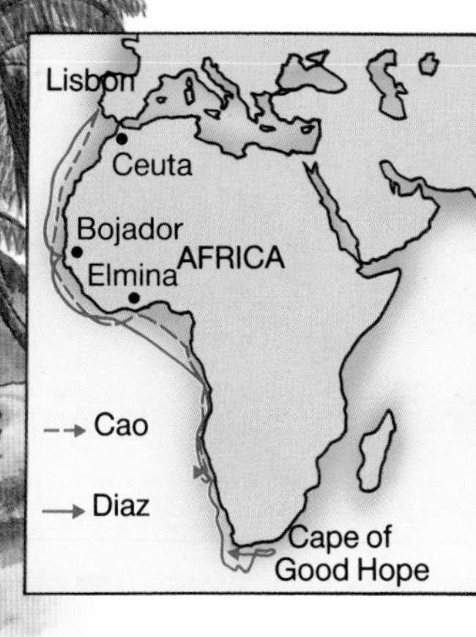

△ The Portuguese pushed their way down the west coast of Africa, exploring and setting up colonies as they went.

Europe at war

In Europe there was a period of almost continuous war. The longest-lasting was between France and England. William the Conqueror's invasion of England in 1066 had united the countries on either side of the English Channel, but there were always power struggles going on. The year 1337 began a century of warfare between the two countries, when Edward III, the king of England, claimed that he was the rightful king of France. In 1356, Edward captured the French king at Poitiers and forced him to concede large areas of France by a treaty signed in 1360. The French began to win back their country after 1429, when the besieged town of Orleans was rescued by an army led by Joan of Arc, a young peasant girl. By 1453 the English held only the port of Calais and the Channel Islands.

Ⓐ THE PORTUGUESE IN AFRICA

The Portuguese wanted to build up their trade with Africa in gold and slaves. But they were afraid of the Muslims, who were already well-established there. The Portuguese captured the North African city of Ceuta in 1415 and then explored the west coast of Africa. By 1482 they had built the first of a series of fortified trading posts, at Elmina. By 1500 there were 10,000 African slaves arriving in the Portuguese capital, Lisbon, each year.

WESTERN EUROPE

1400–8 Welsh revolt against English rule led by Owain Glyndwr.
1406 James I of Scotland held captive in London for 18 years.
1415 English defeat the French at Agincourt.
1423 Outbreak of 30-year war between Milan and Florence.
1431 Joan of Arc burnt at the stake by French clergy who supported the English.
1431 Henry VI of England is crowned King of France in Paris.
1436 French, under Charles VII, take Paris.
1450 Glasgow University founded in reign of James II of Scotland.
1453 Hundred Years' War between England and France comes to an end.
1455-80 Wars between two rival claimants for the throne of England, known as the Wars of the Roses.
1485 Henry Tudor becomes the first Tudor king of England.
1492 Granada, last Muslim stronghold in Spain, reconquered by Christian forces.

N. AND E. EUROPE

1410 Poles defeat the Teutonic Knights at the Battle of Tannenberg.
1437 Albert II of Hapsburg becomes King of Hungary, and of Bohemia and Germany in 1438.
1439 Official separation of the Greek and Russian Orthodox churches.
1445 First printed book (a Bible) in Europe produced by the German Johann Gutenberg.
1453 Constantinople falls to the Ottoman Turks. End of the Byzantine Empire.
1456 Ottomans capture Athens.
1459 Ottomans conquer Serbia.
1460 Ottomans occupy the Greek Peloponnese.
1462 Beginning of the reign of Ivan III of Russia, married to a Byzantine princess, Sophia Palaeologa.
1478 Ottomans conquer Albania.
1478 Ivan III conquers Novgorod.
1480 Ivan III refuses to pay tribute to the Mongols, drives them out of Moscow and declares himself Tsar of Russia.

AFRICA

1415 Portuguese capture the town of Ceuta, North Africa.
1416 Venetians defeat the Ottoman Turks at Gallipoli.
1422 First siege of Constantinople by the Ottoman Turks.
1424 Portuguese colonies on Madeira.
1434 Portuguese explore south of Cape Bojador in Africa.
c1450 Kingdom of Songhai in West Africa. University at the city of Timbuktu.
1451 Beginning of the reign of Mehemed II, Sultan of the Ottoman Turks.
1471 Tangier conquered by the Portuguese.
1482 Portuguese Diogo Cao reaches the mouth of the River Congo.
1487 Portuguese Bartolomeu Diaz sails round the Cape of Good Hope.
1490 King Nzinga Nkuwu of the Congo is baptized a Christian.
1497 Portuguese Vasco da Gama sails to India via the Cape of Good Hope.

ASIA, FAR EAST

c1400 Khmer kingdom of Cambodia collapses.
1405-33 Chinese admiral Cheng Ho's diplomatic voyages to Java, India, Persia, Arabia and Africa.
1409 Chinese general Ch'iu Fu's expedition against the Mongols.
1421 Capital of China moved to Beijing. Great Wall of China extended.
1428 Chinese expelled from Vietnam.
1420-30 China opens trade routes to the west.
1447 The Empire of Timur (Tamerlane) begins to break up.
1448-9 One million people die in rebellion against Ming Dynasty rule in China.
1449 Chinese invasion of Mongolia, emperor taken captive.
1471 Vietnam extends its power south.
1477 Beginning of wars between the provinces in Japan lasting 100 years.
1498 First description of a toothbrush in a Chinese encyclopedia.
1500 Empire of Vijayanagara controls southern India.

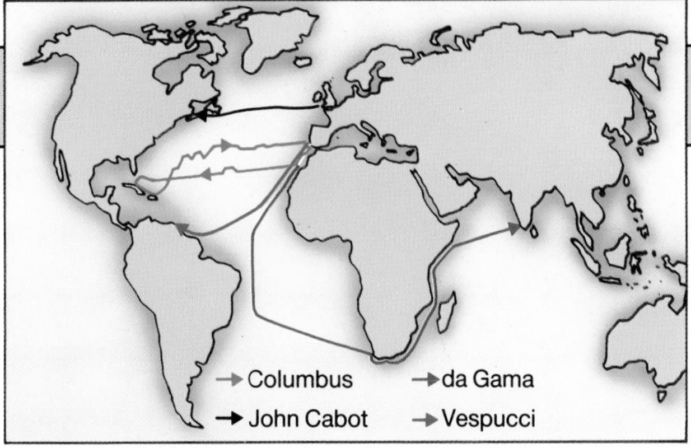

◁ The first voyages of discovery were made in search of new places to trade. Later, Europeans set out to conquer parts of the New World.

EXPLORERS AND DISCOVERY

Several European countries began to make voyages of discovery in the 15th century. In 1497, Portuguese sailors, under Vasco da Gama, were the first to round the Cape of Good Hope in southern Africa and then sail on to India. Here they came into contact with merchants from China and ships called junks. Christopher Columbus was employed by Spain to find a sea route to India and China. Sailing westwards, he came across the West Indies in 1492. An English expedition, led by an Italian navigator called John Cabot, sailed across the Atlantic Ocean and reached Newfoundland (now in Canada) in 1497. Europeans called these territories in the west the New World. Portugal and Spain decided, in 1494, to divide up this world between them.

▽ Christopher Columbus was an Italian from Genoa, who, in 1492, was employed by Spain to find a westerly route to India.

DISCOVERIES

Portugal
1397 Canary Islands
1415 Ceuta conquered.
1420 Madeira.
1427 The Azores.
1460 Sierra Leone.
1487 Bartolomeu Diaz reaches the Cape of Good Hope.
1498 Vasco da Gama reaches India.
1500 Brazil.
1510 Goa.
1528 Mombasa.

Spain
1492 Columbus reaches the West Indies and in 1502 Mexico.

Italy
1499 Vespucci reaches South America, explores the mouth of the River Amazon and goes north to the West Indies.

England
1497 John Cabot leads an expedition to explore the coast of Nova Scotia to Newfoundland.

THE AMERICAS

c1400 Settlements from Norway abandoned in Greenland.
1428 Alliance formed by three cities gives Aztecs control of Valley of Mexico.
1438-63 First large-scale extension of Inca Empire.
1440-68 Aztec rule of Montezuma I extends to the Gulf of Mexico.
1463-71 Inca emperor Topa Inca conquers the north coastal lands of Peru. Chimu kingdom destroyed.
1486-1502 Aztec Empire reaches Pacific coast and Guatemala.
1492 Christopher Columbus reaches the Bahamas from Europe and establishes a base at Hispaniola.
1493 Beginning of Inca expansion north to Colombia. Second Inca capital built at Quito.
1494 Treaty allows Spain and Portugal to divide the New World between them.
1499-1502 Amerigo Vespucci explores South American coast. The Americas are named after him.

TIMECHART 1

WORLD RELIGIONS

The period covered in this book saw the rise of a number of religions across the world. There are some that we know very little about today but most are still important religions.

Christianity
The followers of Jesus Christ spread the religion of Christianity throughout the Roman world, despite fierce opposition from the authorities and much persecution. In 312 the Roman Emperor Constantine made it the official religion of the Romans. Christianity was spread by missionaries who established Christian communities, churches and monasteries. In the late 11th century western Christians began Crusades against the Muslims in the eastern Mediterranean. At first they joined with the Christian Byzantine Empire, but different views soon developed. In 1054 the Church divided, after disagreements between Pope Leo IX and the patriarch of Constantinople. The Orthodox Christian Church made its base in Constantinople, and the Catholic Church was based in Rome.

Islam
Islam means 'submitting to God'. It was the creation of Muhammad, born in Mecca in 570. He began to preach that there was only one, true God. After Muhammad's flight to the city of Medina he set up a Muslim community and, by the time of his death in 632, nearly all of his native Arabia had been converted to the religion of Islam. The followers of Islam, the Muslims, extended their religion and their empire by force until they became a threat to the established civilizations of the Mediterranean and Europe. Even as late as 1571, Christian states united in a 'Holy League'against the Muslims and fought the Battle of Lepanto in western Greece in which they defeated the Turkish fleet.

Buddhism
The religion founded by Siddartha Gautama Buddha around 566 BC is still practiced by millions across the world today. It is based on the idea of 'karma', that is, that a person's good or bad deeds produce either rewards or punishments in this life or in lives to come through reincarnation (coming back to life as another person or an animal). After the Buddha's death in 483 BC, some of his followers formed an order of Buddhist monks to spread his preaching and ideas. The Buddhist religion spread mainly in the East.

AFRICA

c400 First towns established south of the Sahara.
429 Vandals invade Roman province of North Africa.
c450 Nok people in West Africa using iron.
c500 Arrival in southern Africa of Bantu people, using iron and driving cattle.
533 Successful Roman campaign against the Vandals.
600 Kingdom of Ghana, first state in West Africa.
618 Persians conquer Egypt.
698 Arabs conquer Carthage on North African coast. African coastal people converted to Islam.

Bronze pot from West Africa c. 9th century.

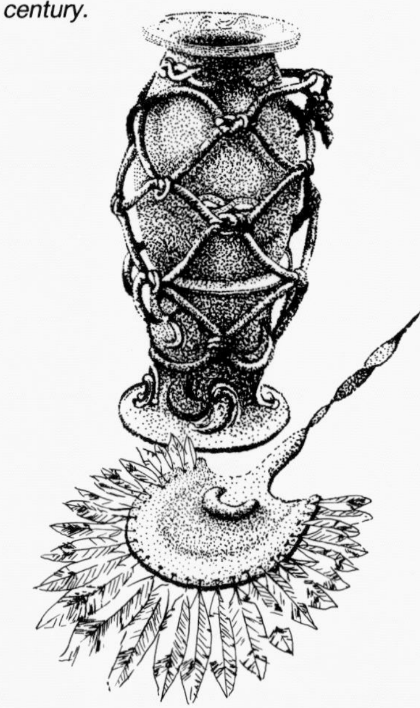

Fan with copper holder from West Africa c. 9th century.

700 Arabs trading with African cities south of the Sahara Desert.
711 Muslims in control of whole of North Africa.
788 Muslim dynasty of Idrisid rules in Morocco.
800 West African kingdoms established. Trade north of the Sahara Desert.
909 Fatamid Dynasty takes over Arab kingdoms in North Africa.
999 Bagauda is the first king of Kano in Nigeria.
c1000 Islamic influence spreads into West Africa and up the River Nile into Nubia.
c1000 West African trading towns well established.

EUROPE

c450 Saxons, Angles and Jutes begin to settle in Britain.
451 Attila the Hun's forces defeated in north-eastern France.
455 Rome sacked by the Vandals.
475–6 Romulus Augustulus last Roman emperor in the west.
488 Ostrogoths invade Italy.
493 Theodoric, the Ostrogoth, establishes his capital at Ravenna, Italy.
527 Justinian crowned Emperor with his wife Theodora in Constantinople.
534 Slavs and Bulgars attack the Eastern Roman Empire.
552 Eastern Roman Empire forces reoccupy southern Spain.
560 Irish monk. Columba, founds a church on Iona, Scotland.
568 Lombards invade Italy.
597 Pope Gregory I sends Augustine to convert the English.
613 Jerusalem falls to the Persians.
625 Sutton Hoo ship burial. Death of Raedwald, High King of Britain.

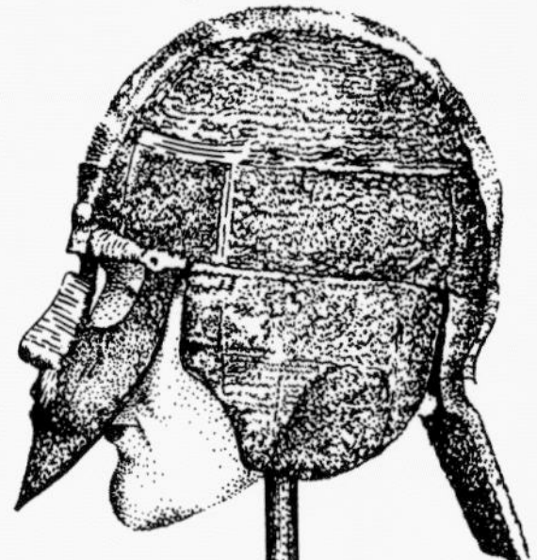

Helmet from Sutton Hoo, 625.

664 Synod of Whitby establishes that the Church in England follows the Roman Church of the Pope.
674-8 Constantinople beseiged by Muslim armies.
697 Byzantine rule in North Africa taken over by Muslims.
698 Lindisfarne Gospels are the first psalms produced in the language of the Anglo-Saxons.
717 Beginning of struggle in Byzantium for and against the use of religious images – icons.
751 Pepin III founds the Carolingian Dynasty in France.
771 Charlemagne becomes sole ruler of the Franks.
787 Council of Nicaea restores use of icons in churches.
793 First recorded Viking raid on England.
795 Franks create frontier zones in Spain and Pannonia.
800 Charlemagne crowned Emperor of Holy Roman Empire by the Pope.
862 Christian mission to Moravia.
966 State of Poland founded.

ASIA AND RUSSIA

480 Huns invade the Gupta Empire in India.
c550 Avars driven out of Mongolia.
c600 Hun invasion in East recedes as Huns are attacked by the Persians and the Turks.
600 Power of the Pallava people established in southern India.
715 Muslim armies conquer Sind in north-east India.
736 Founding of the city of Dhillika, the first city of Delhi.
740 Pallava power destroyed by Chalukya people in southern India.
751 Muslims defeat a Chinese army in central Asia.
862 Rurik the Viking founds Novgorod in Russia.

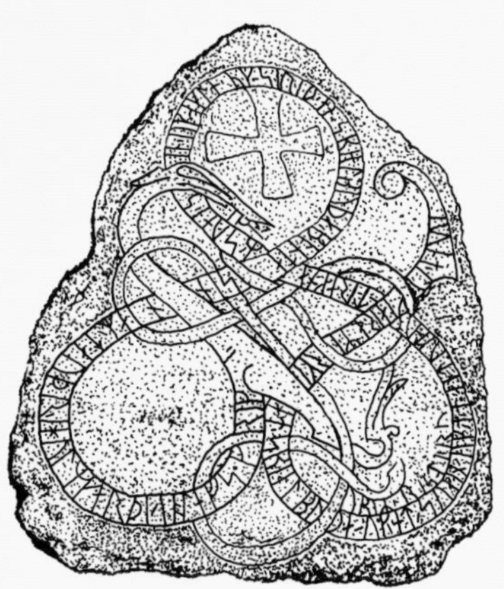

Viking carved boulder, Sweden c. 850.

866 Beginning of conversion of Russia to Christianity.
957 Christianity spreads through Russia.
978 Russian state founded and based in Kiev.
985 Chola kingdom in India.

AMERICAS

c500 Farming introduced into the forests of Brazil.
500 Thule hunters arrive in Alaska.
600 City of Tiahuanaco, religious centre in the Andes.
c600 Mayan civilization at its height.

Mayan stone sacred image c. 650.

600–800 Towns and cities built along river valleys in North America.
650–750 City of Teotihuacan in decline.
700 Mayan city of Tikal rebuilt.
700 Anasazi people in American south-west begin to build large settlements.

Hand-eye motif of Anasazi people, c. 750.

800–900 Mayan civilization in decline.
800 Bow and arrow first used in North America.
800 Mogollon people in New Mexico build farming villages.
800 Dorset Inuit hunters in Greenland and north-east Canada.
900 Anasazi farmers build pueblos – cliff dwellings.
947 Birth of Quetzalcoatl, considered a god by the Aztecs.
950 Toltec city of Tula founded.
984 Vikings reach Greenland from Iceland and found colonies.
c1000 Northern Iroquoian villages spread to St Lawrence River and the eastern Great Lakes.
c1000 Viking settlements in Labrador and Newfoundland.

CHINA AND AUSTRALASIA

c400 Easter Island and Hawaii islands settled by Polynesians.
c500 Period of the Six Dynasties in China. Toba Wei empire established in northern China.
552 Buddhist religion introduced into Japan from China.
581 China reunified under General Yang Chien, who founds the Sui Dynasty.
605–610 Canal dug to join the Yangtze and Huanh Ho rivers in China.
606 First written examination for Chinese civil service entrants.
607 Tibet becomes a unified state.
618 Beginning of the Tang Dynasty in China.

Pottery camel from Tang dynasty, c. 700.

624 Buddhism becomes the official religion of China.
645 Buddhism reaches Tibet.
650 Polynesian Islands, except for New Zealand, settled.
695 Mongols invade China.
844 Buddhists persecuted in China.
868 World's first printed book produced in China.
907 Mongol expansion into Inner Mongolia and northern China.
939 Vietnam becomes independent of China.
960 Sung Dynasty unites central and southern China.
c1000 New Zealand first settled.
c1000 Enormous head-statues erected on Easter Island.
c1000 Chinese use gunpowder in war.

TIMECHART 2

RECORDS AND WRITING

The written evidence of past peoples is an important source for historians to study, but sometimes this evidence is difficult to understand. The Mayan people of South America used a system of dates which we can decipher today, even though their calendar starts at our equivalent of 3114 BC. However, we still find it difficult to understand some of their writing. The Maya used 'glyphs' (pictures) to indicate words or phrases.

Much of the written evidence for the medieval period can easily be understood today. Documents, inscriptions and records can be translated whether written in Latin, Arabic or Chinese script.

Latin, the language of the Romans, was used throughout their empire and even replaced native languages in some of their provinces. Latin was also the official language for the Christian Church in the west from Anglo-Saxon times. So much Latin has passed into the English language that over half our words are derived from it. Other languages in western Europe also show a strong Latin influence, for example French, Spanish and Italian. Here is one word:

Latin familia
English family
Italian famiglia
Spanish familia
French famille

Many peoples use the word July (or something similar – in French *Juillet*, in Italian *Luglio*). All these words come from the Roman name for the seventh month, taken from Julius Caesar. The 'Arabic' numbers that we use today are adapted from those originally invented by the Gupta people of India and brought to the west by Arab merchants.

The remnants of languages used by past peoples are also found in place-names. In England the Anglo-Saxon peoples have left us names like Chelmsford (ford = river crossing) and Boxworth (worth = land enclosed by a hedge). The Vikings left us with endings for place names such as -thorpe (= small settlement) or -wick (= bay or inlet).

There was also an influence from the Byzantine Empire which can still be seen today. The Greek language was emphasized by the Emperor Heraclius when he came to power in 610. Christian missions by St Cyril and St Method came to Moravia in 862. St Cyril changed his Greek language to adapt it to native speakers, and the Cyrillic alphabet, still used in some Slav countries such as Russia, comes from this root.

AFRICA

1052 Islamic forces attacks Ghana.
1054 Muslim conquest of West Africa.
1171 Saladin founds his Ayyubid Dynasty.
c1200 Rock-cut churches built in Ethiopia.
1200 Rise of the Kingdom of Mali, West Africa.
1200 City-states of Hausa in Nigeria founded.
c1250 Berbers establish a number of states in North Africa. Known as the Barbary Coast by Europeans.
c1300 Rise of the Kingdom of Benin in Nigeria.
1324 Mansa Musa, King of Mali, in West Africa, visits Cairo.
1397 Portuguese reach the Canary Islands.
1415 Portuguese capture the town of Ceuta, North Africa, and begin voyages around African coasts.
1434 Portuguese explore south of Cape Bojador.
1445 Portuguese reach the mouth of the River Congo.
c1450 Kingdom of Songhai in West Africa. University at the city of Timbuktu.
1471 Tangier conquered by the Portuguese.
1487 Bartolomeu Diaz sails around the Cape of Good Hope.
1497 Portuguese Vasco da Gama sails to India via the Cape of Good Hope.

Vasco da Gama, 1462–1524.

EUROPE

1016 Danish King Canute rules England, Denmark and Norway.
1066 Normans invade England.

Bayeux Tapestry, c. 1080.

1096 First western Christian Crusade against the Muslims in the Holy Land.
1099 Jerusalem captured by Crusaders.
1119 University of Bologna founded.
1187 Saladin, Muslim leader, recaptures Jerusalem.
c1200s Building of Gothic style cathedrals.
1202 Arabic numerals introduced into Europe.
1215 English barons force King John to sign the *Magna Carta*.
1309 Pope moves residence from Rome to Avignon, France.
1337 Start of Hundred Years' War between England and France.
1347 Black Death begins to sweep through Europe.
c1350 Firearms first used in Europe.
1358 Peasants' rebellion in France.
1381 Peasants' revolt in England.
1415 English defeat the French at the Battle of Agincourt.
1428 Joan of Arc begins campaigning against English forces in France.
1431 Joan of Arc burned at the stake.
1445 First printed book produced in Europe.

Book illustration, France c. 1485.

1453 Constantinople falls to the Ottoman Turks.
1455–80 Wars of the Roses in England.
1492 Granada, last Muslim stronghold in Spain, reconquered by Christian forces.

ASIA AND RUSSIA

1054 Kievan Russia in decline, invasion of nomads from Asia.
1162 Temujin (later called Genghis Khan) born.

Genghis Khan, 1162–1227.

1206 Muslim sultanate founded in Delhi, India.
1206 Mongol tribes united by Genghis Khan.
1227 Genghis Khan dies. Mongol Empire divided between his four sons.
1236 Mongols destroy the Kama Bulgars.
1242 Mongol Golden Horde established in southern Russia.
1328 Duke Ivan I begins the expansion of Moscow.
c1341 Black Death begins in Asia.
1439 Official separation of the Greek and Russian Orthodox Churches.

Ivan III, 1440–1505.

1480 Ivan III refuses to pay Mongol tribute and declares himself Tsar of Russia.
1500 Empire of Vijayanagara controls southern India.

AMERICAS

1100 Anasazi people build settlements in protected places.
1150 Anasazi now most powerful people in the American South-west.
c1200 Decline of Mayan civilization in the Yucatan Peninsula of Mesoamerica.
1200 Legendary foundation of first Inca city, Cuzco.
c1200 Beginnings of Aztec power.
c1300 Pueblo cliff settlements abandoned.
1345 Rise of Aztec civilization.
1438 Beginning of large-scale extension of Inca Empire.

Inca record-keeping strings, c. 1450.

1492 Christopher Columbus reaches the Bahamas.
1494 Spain and Portugal divide the New World between themselves.
1499 Amerigo Vespucci begins his exploration of South American coast. The Americas are named after him.

Christopher Columbus, 1451–1506.

CHINA AND AUSTRALASIA

1044 Foundation of first Burmese state.
1211 Genghis Khan leads Mongol invasion of China.
1215 Peking captured by Mongols.
1264 Kublai Khan founds the Tuan Dynasty in China.
1275 Marco Polo arrives in China from Venice.
1279 Mongols conquer southern China.
1307 First Christian archbishop in Peking.

Maori necklace, c. 1300.

c1350 Maori people in New Zealand build fortified settlements.
1368 Ming Dynasty founded in China.

Porcelain vase from Ming Dynasty c. 1380.

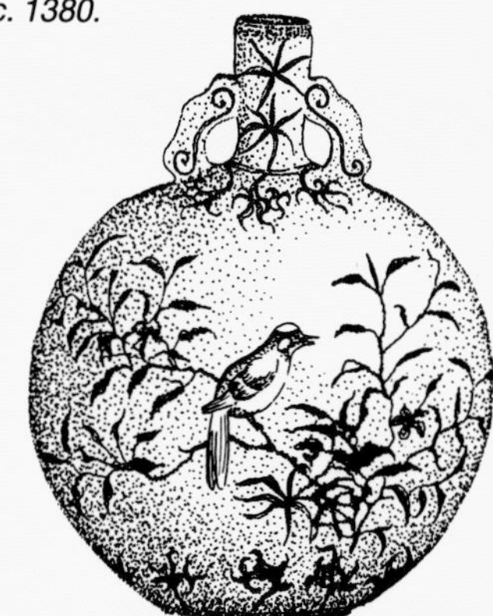

c1400 Khmer kingdom of Cambodia collapses.
1421 Capital of China moved to Peking.
1428 Chinese expelled from Vietnam.
1477 Beginning of wars between the provinces in Japan lasting nearly 100 years.
1498 First description of a toothbrush in a Chinese encyclopedia.

GLOSSARY

AD The abbreviated form of *'Anno Domini'* used for dates.

archaeologist A scientist who collects and interprets evidence from the past which survives under or on the ground.

'barbarians' The name given to foreigners by both Romans and Byzantines.

BC The abbreviated form of 'Before Christ' used for dates.

Black Death The plague that swept through much of Europe in the 14th century.

Bretwalda The title, meaning 'High King' in Anglo-Saxon Britain.

Buddhism The religion founded by Siddhartha Gautama.

Byzantine Empire An extension of the Eastern Roman Empire with its capital at Constantinople.

caliphs The leaders of the early Islamic dynasties.

Christianity The religion of the followers of Jesus Christ who died AD 29.

church The building for the worship of **Christianity**.

civilization An organized society with its own identity, sufficiently wealthy to have influence over a large territory.

colony A settlement of people establishing their way of life outside their own country.

Crusades Religious wars by Christians against **Muslims**.

dynasty The ruling family of a king or emperor in which power passes from one generation to another.

empire A large territory ruled over by an emperor or a king and extending far beyond the ruler's homeland.

frontier A boundary of a territory or empire, often defended by forts.

Golden Horde A Mongol **horde** set up in Russia by Genghis Khan's great-nephew to serve as both a fighting force and mobile administration center.

Holy Land Place where Jesus Christ lived and claimed by Christians as their own.

horde A group of tribes of people originating in the Russian **steppes**.

infidel Term meaning 'unbeliever' used of the **Muslims** by Christians.

inscription Writing cut into stone or metal, for official purposes.

Islam Religion founded by the Prophet Muhammad (died in 632).

kayak A type of boat used first by the Thule people of the Arctic.

keep The strongest building inside a medieval castle.

khan The leader of a nomadic horde. The most famous was Genghis Khan, the Mongol leader.

marches Frontier lands created as buffer zones between the Franks and their enemies.

Mesoamerica The area of land between North and South America (from Mexico to Panama).

migration The movement of peoples to new lands.

monastery The place where communities of monks or nuns lived and worshipped.

motte and bailey A type of wooden and earth castle introduced into England by the Normans.

mosque The place for Muslims to meet for study and prayer.

Muslim A follower of the religion of **Islam**.

New World The name given to the Americas by Europeans.

nomads People whose way of life keeps them moving across their territory without making permanent **settlements**.

patriarch A head of the Christian Orthodox Church.

pilgrimage A journey made by a religious person to a holy place.

Pope The leader of the western Christians, based in Rome.

province A conquered land governed as part of an **empire**.

settlement A place where people live and build houses.

shogun Military dictator in Japan.

slaves People who are forced to work for someone against their will.

steppes Russian name for huge areas of grassland plains.

sultan The title of the **Muslim** leader, used by the Seljuk Turks.

INDEX